THE OPEN BOOK SERIES

UNDERWATER LIFE

Edited by Tessa Bridger

Algae – Sponges and Coelenterates – Water Insects – Molluscs – Shellfish – Crustaceans – Turtles – Amphibians – Life in the River – Fish of the Sea – Freshwater Fish

HODDER AND STOUGHTON
LONDON SYDNEY AUCKLAND TORONTO

British Library Cataloguing in Publication Data

Bridger, Tessa
    Underwater life. – (The open book series)
    1. Aquatic animals – Juvenile literature
    I. Title
    591.92   QL120

ISBN 0-340-33938-1
ISBN 0-340-33009-0 (Pbk)

Copyright © 1981 Gruppo Editoriale Fabbri S.p.A., Milano – Le Livre de Paris S.A. – Hachette, Bagneux.

English language edition copyright © 1984 Hodder and Stoughton Ltd.

First published in this edition in Great Britain 1984.

Published by Hodder and Stoughton Children's Books, a division of Hodder and Stoughton Ltd, Mill Road, Dunton Green, Sevenoaks, Kent TN13 2YJ.

Photoset by Rowland Phototypesetting Ltd, Bury St Edmunds, Suffolk.

Printed in Belgium by Henri Proost et Cie, Turnhout.

Algae

Algae are everywhere. They are under rocks, in streams and rivers and in the sea. They first appeared on the Earth about three billion years ago. They are an essential part of plankton which is the most basic part of the food chain and are, therefore, essential to man's survival. Man uses algae as medicine and, in some parts of the world, algae are part of the staple diet. What are they, these plants that have diversified into an amazing number of species? What exactly are algae?

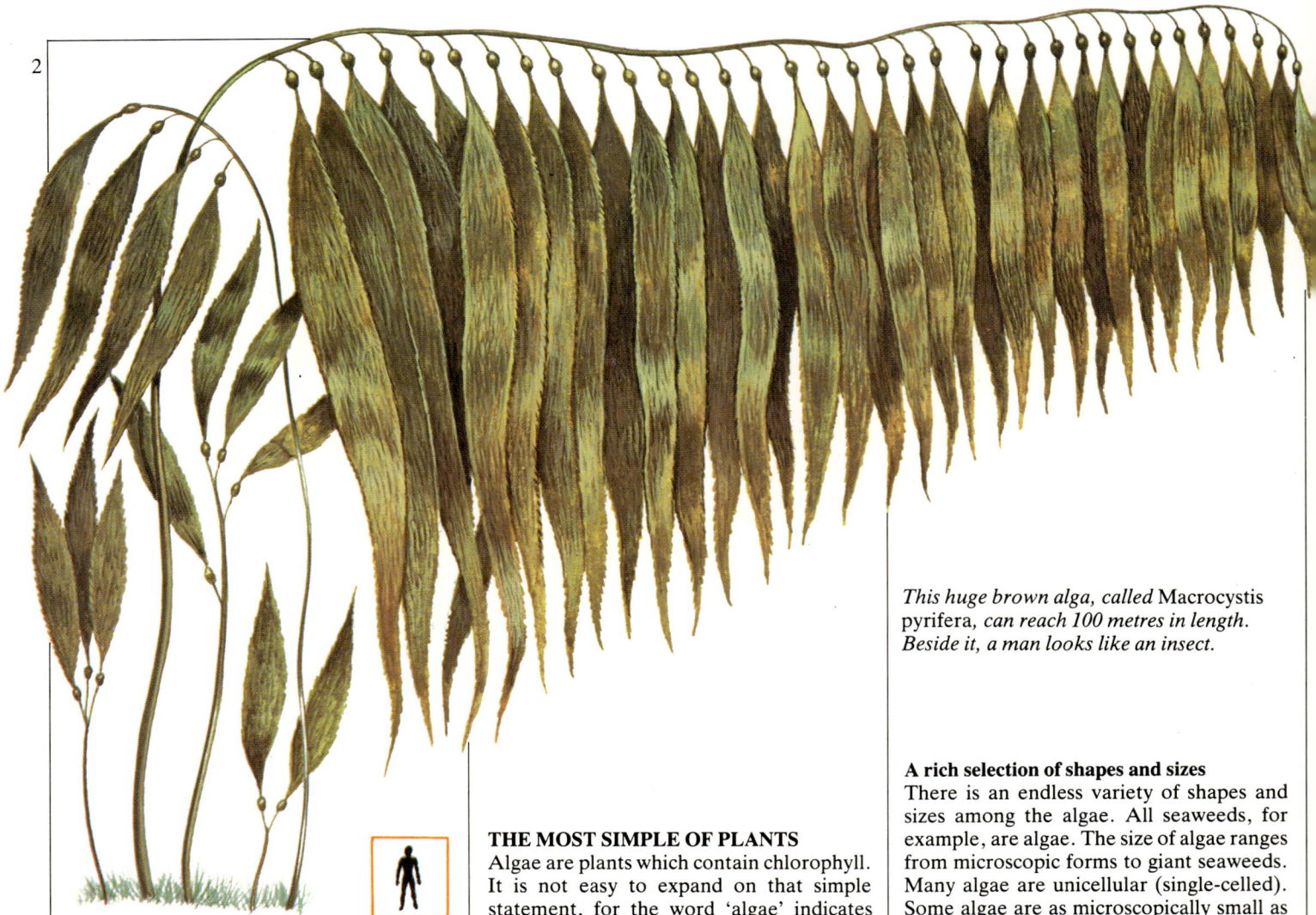

This huge brown alga, called Macrocystis pyrifera, *can reach 100 metres in length. Beside it, a man looks like an insect.*

THE MOST SIMPLE OF PLANTS

Algae are plants which contain chlorophyll. It is not easy to expand on that simple statement, for the word 'algae' indicates an extremely rich group of vegetable species (over 20,000) which are very different both in shape and way of living.

It is difficult to classify algae in the way that other plants are classified. Modern systematics does not consider them to be a single group. For ease, botanists have classified algae according to colour. There are four main groups: the green algae (Chlorophyceae); the brown algae (Phaeophyceae); the red algae (Rhodophyceae); the blue-green algae (Cyanophyceae).

Further, botanists say that 'algae' is a collective name for diverse groups of vegetables which have some characteristics in common. These characteristics are:
1. Algae have no roots, stalks or real leaves or flowers.
2. The cells are much closer together than in other species of plants. The simple body of the algae is called the *thallus*. For this reason algae belong to a division called Thallophyta, which also includes fungi and bacteria (which contain no chlorophyll).
3. Most algae live in water, both sea and fresh water.
4. Because algae contain chlorophyll, they make their food in the same way as the more superior plants which have complicated root systems. Algae are the most simple of the green plants producing oxygen.

A rich selection of shapes and sizes

There is an endless variety of shapes and sizes among the algae. All seaweeds, for example, are algae. The size of algae ranges from microscopic forms to giant seaweeds. Many algae are unicellular (single-celled). Some algae are as microscopically small as bacteria and there can be millions in one drop of water. Algae can be oval, spherical, disc-shaped, box-shaped, filament-shaped or rod-shaped.

Some algae have one or more flagella (tail-like propellers), which permit them to move as if they were animals; others are covered in mineral salts, forming a sort of shell which is perforated and regular in shape.

At the other end of the scale, there are gigantic algae, fixed to the seabed by organs similar to roots. These can reach lengths of from 90 metres to 100 metres and weigh several hundred kilogrammes. An example of this is the enormous brown alga shown above. You can get some idea of its size when you compare it with the man alongside.

Between these two extremes there is an enormous range of plants of various sizes and shapes. There are many algae that look like simple pieces of wire; others are blade-shaped and could be mistaken for leaves. Some brown algae like the bladder-wracks (*Fucus*), the gulf weeds and the species shown above are equipped with spherical bladders which, in certain cases, could be mistaken for fruits. These bladders are, in fact, cavities full of air and serve as floating lungs!

Where they live

As we have seen, algae are simple plants living in aquatic environments (although not all aquatic plants are algae). Most live in the sea, but there are some freshwater algae living in lakes, rivers, puddles, swamps, ditches, streams, ponds, pools and some are even found in drops of dew. But whether in the sea or fresh water, algae help to make up the many tons of plankton – the groups of microscopic organisms both plant (phytoplankton) and animal (zooplankton) – which are suspended in the water in their billions.

Plankton is a rich source of food for higher animals. It is the first stage in the food chain of the sea, in fact the tiny single-celled diatoms are sometimes called 'the grass of the sea'. The primary consumers are the zooplankton, and fish, from sprats to sharks, are the secondary consumers.

Some algae are not really aquatic at all and need only a damp environment in which to survive. Some live in mud, others live in the humid ground of fields and woods, in the snow, on damp rocks and walls, on tree bark and on leaves. There are parasitic algae that live on other algae, or on fungi, or on the cells and in the blood of animals (man included). Many species of algae live in close association (symbiosis) with various species of fungi, with which they create vegetation called lichens.

In the sea, algae are found near the surface where the sunlight reaches. Thanks to their special pigments, the brown and red algae can make better use of the sun's rays and are able to reach greater depths.

A PLANT IN SUNLIGHT – AN ANIMAL IN THE DARK

Euglena is a common genus of unicellular algae most often found in water polluted with urban wastes. There are many species of Euglena.

When the environment in which it lives is exposed to the sun, the Euglena is green with chlorophyll and able to get the nutriment it needs by photosynthesis, behaving exactly like a plant. However, when the Euglena lives in the dark, it loses its chlorophyll and 'whitens'. In this state it is forced to obtain the organic substances it needs from outside, behaving more like an animal than a plant.

Other algae also behave like this and thus confirm that it is very hard for us to distinguish plants from animals among these simple organisms.

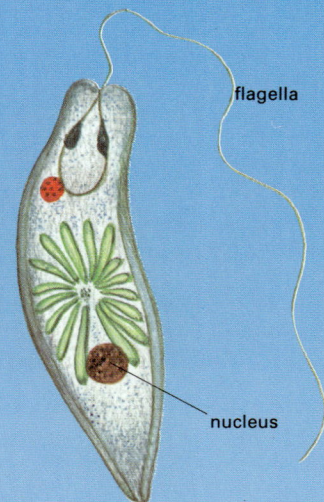

flagella

nucleus

How they live

All algae are self-supporting. This means that because they contain chlorophyll, they are able to build up food supplies from materials in their surroundings. They do this by absorbing water and carbon dioxide through their bodies. They do not possess real leaves and roots because they do not need them.

The other two groups in the division Thallophyta, fungi and bacteria, have no chlorophyll and are not able to manufacture their own living substances. They are, therefore, either parasites (living off other living plants or animals) or saprophytes (living off dead organic matter).

How algae reproduce

Algae can reproduce in numerous different ways. Reproduction often takes place through the simple fragmentation of the thallus, with spores or with special buds called bulbils. Some also reproduce sexually; in this case male and female cells are emitted; the male cells penetrate the female cells and fertilise them. They in turn begin the growth of new organisms. The most complex life cycles occur in the red algae. Algae, although individually inconspicuous, can multiply rapidly enough to colour the water. The Red Sea is sometimes said to get its name from the vast quantity of a reddish, blue-green algae found in it.

green algae

brown algae

red algae

phytoplankton

zooplankton

pelagic fauna (surface dwellers)

abyssal fauna (deep water dwellers)

4

ALGAE GROUPS
The endless variety of algae are usually gathered in four main groups and are sometimes further subdivided according to the genus.

Cyanophyceae
These are the blue-green algae. They are the oldest and most simple algae. The cells do not have a real nucleus. It seems that they were the first of all living organisms to carry out the photosynthesis function. They live in the sea and in fresh water and also on the land on damp rocks.

Chlorophyceae
These are the green algae which can either be very simple unicellular species or fairly complex pluricellular species. The most highly evolved of all algae belong to this group. Most microscopic green algae live in fresh water, but there is a greater variety of shapes among marine species. Some of them are similar to tiny umbrellas. Others are like thin filaments, either single or in tufts, and yet others are like leaves. Such a one is the *Ulva* which is similar in appearance to a lettuce leaf.

Phaephyceae
In the thallus of the brown algae there are often rhizoids (formations similar to roots), which hold the plant firmly on to the seabed; a part similar to a stalk (coloid), and parts similar to leaves. Bladders full of air used as floating lungs can be seen in many species, such as the gulf weed and the huge *Macrocystis*. They also include the kelps and dense, floating masses of seaweed found in the Sargasso Sea.

Rhodophyceae
The red algae. Some can be up to 40 centimetres long but most are delicate seaweeds. Some are branched and in the shape of small bushes. Their colour ranges from a pale pink to a deep, reddish-purple. The presence of special pigments hides the green colour of the chlorophyll, and allow red algae to make efficient use of sunlight and live at greater depths than other algae.

The red waters of Lake Tovel, in Italy, are caused by a microscopic species of phyrophyte, Glenodinum sanguineum, *which produces numerous grains of red pigment.*

Women shopping for algae at a market in Zamboanga, in the Philippines.

ALGAE FOR SALADS, DESSERTS, ICE-CREAMS AND COSMETICS
Anyone who goes to Japan, or even eats in a Japanese restaurant, will come across the edible algae. A red algae similar to a lettuce is grown and gathered on the rocks at low tide. Cooked and served with soy sauce, these algae have been eaten for many years. Many other species are also good to eat and are found on the table in Oriental countries.

But it is not only the Orientals that eat algae, Europeans and Americans do too. In Scotland, an edible seaweed called kelp is collected from the shore and cooked until it forms a junket, which is considered a great delicacy. Carragheen is another edible variety, and is used for making soup and a kind of blancmange; and yet another is laver, used in the preparation of laver bread.

Some substances extracted from red algae are used to thicken liquids, including milk. These substances can be used in preparing desserts, jams, jellies and cosmetics, and are a type of vegetable gelatine. One substance used for thickening is agar-agar, which is extracted from red algae from the Pacific. In all the laboratories where research on microbes is carried out, these microscopic organisms are bred on a culture soup of agar-agar.

Special powders called alginates are extracted from brown algae. We probably do not think of algae when eating an ice-cream. However, ice-cream owes its creamy consistency to an alginate which is mixed in with the other ingredients and prevents the ice-cream from melting too quickly. Alginic acid is a substance used commercially in the manufacture of a number of products, including adhesives and textiles.

On the coasts of France, algae are reaped during low tide as if they were grass. They are then used as fodder for livestock or, in some cases, as fertilisers.

In many major groups of algae the members have lime or silicon deposits, either in the cell walls or as a form of external shell. These are readily preserved as fossils. Fossil diatoms provide abrasives and are used for making toothpaste, filters and insulating materials.

Euglenophytes

These are unicellular planktonic algae which have one or more flagella. They live in any body of water, from a puddle to an ocean. Some species of this group are adapted to a parasitic life, like the trypanosome which causes sleeping sickness and which is often classified among animals in the group of protozoans. A well-known species is the *Euglena* shown on page three.

Pyrrophytes

These are also called fire algae and are unicellular and planktonic. They often have appendages similar to wings or horns and have two flagella. They live in the sea and fresh water. In Japan the cultivation of pyrrophytes, on nets supported on frames, is a large and important industry.

Above: one of the best known members of the group of chlorophytes (green algae), the sea lettuce (Ulva lactuca) *which is very common.*

Right: a fucus (Fucus vesiculosus). *The wavy bubbles which can be seen on the 'leaves' of this alga are air bladders, little sacs of air which help it to float. The fucus is a brown alga. The order of fucoids that it belongs to includes the largest of all algae.*

Below: a specimen of the Gelidium corneum, *which is widespread in the Mediterranean and which belongs to the group of Rhodophyceae, or red algae.*

Bacillarophytes

These unicellular planktonic algae in the division Rhodophyceae are also called diatoms. Their bodies are protected by a wrapping rich in silica and vary in shape from species to species. They live in enormous quantities in the sea and in fresh water. In the sea they make up almost all the total of phytoplankton. Some freshwater species form the mud-coloured slimes found on beds of ponds and leaves of waterplants.

Fossil diatom deposits 916 metres (3,000 feet) thick have been found. Such fossilised forms can given an indication of the ages of the groups to which they belong. Among sea algae, the calcareous corallines were developed 500 million years ago and arose many millions of years before that.

Chrysophytes

These are also called golden algae. They are chiefly unicellular and often have flagella. They are varied in form and live in the sea and fresh water. The unicellular varieties are a golden colour, but the multi-cellular forms are usually a yellowish-green.

Sponges and Coelenterates

On a calm sea shore the tide has washed in a number of strange multi-coloured objects. At first sight they look like delicately patterned parasols . . . but something is not quite right. On closer observation it can be noticed that the objects slowly pulsate . . . they are living beings. Any attempt at capturing them would soon show that the creatures are perfectly capable of defending themselves because they can sting. These objects are, in fact, jellyfish, animals in the Coelenterata group. Some of them give nasty stings, the shock of which can cause swimmers to drown. The related sea-wasp, which is found in the waters off Eastern Australia, has a sting which is fatal.

TWIGS, BRANCHES, FLOWERS, CUSHIONS AND BALLOONS

In the sea and in fresh water, there are, besides fish, crustaceans, molluscs, anemones and starfish, many other animals. Some are so imprecise in shape that it is often difficult to be sure that they are animals just by looking at them.

Good examples of this are the elegant 'twigs' and 'bushes' of corals such as madrepores and sea fans; or the misleading flower-shaped structure of the actinia, commonly called sea anemones; or the vague cushion-shapes of sponges and the delicate 'parasols' of the jellyfish which are perhaps the prettiest of all the sea creatures.

What do these organisms have in common, apart from the fact that they all look like plants and bear little resemblance to animals, and they all live in the same environment? What makes them similar is the fact that they are all primitive animals and, in spite of their varied and beautiful appear-

ances, they are all very simple in structure.

If the observer ignored the tentacles and the complicated ornamentation, he would soon discover that these animals are basically sack-like in structure without the true organs associated with less primitive animals. The walls of the sponge's sack have thousands of microscopic holes, while corals, sea anemones and jellyfish have smooth body walls.

The sponges belong to the phylum Porifera. The word 'poriferous' means having pores. Because of their structure, the pores act like living filters and take in nutriment from the water.

Jellyfish, corals and anemones all belong to the phylum Coelenterata. They have one single opening through which they absorb food and expel wastes.

Jellyfish must move constantly because they are slightly denser than seawater. If they stop moving, the jellyfish sink away from the habitat of their normal prey.

PROTOZOANS AND METAZOANS

Protozoa are single-celled animals, and from a zoological point of view, are very important, for they represent the development from the single-celled animals of the microscopic protozoans (which includes amoeba), to the pluricellular Metazoa which are larger and more complicated animals. They were completely unknown until 1674 when a Dutchman, Anton van Leeuwenhoek, observed them under his home-made microscope.

The word *Protozoa* means 'first animals' and these single-celled creatures were probably the first organisms to inhabit the earth and would have played a significant part in the evolution of all other life. Metazoans comprise all the animals above the protozoans. These organisms, which originated from a single cell, are composed of many cells.

While in the protozoan the single cell carries out all the vital functions, the various cells in the metazoan are specialised in their functions. Sponges and coelenterates, which are the most primitive metazoans, show the first stage of this specialisation because their cells are differentiated, but have still not succeeded in forming precise organs. This type of organisation characterises most other metazoans, and in some cases is extremely complex.

In the sketch on the right is a comparison between the different types of organisation associated with, firstly, a protozoan, secondly, a sponge which is a very primitive metazoan and thirdly, man, a particularly highly evolved metazoan.

Paramecium (Protozoa)

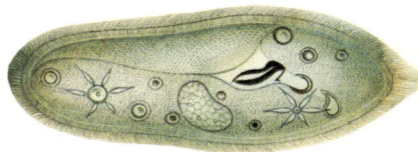

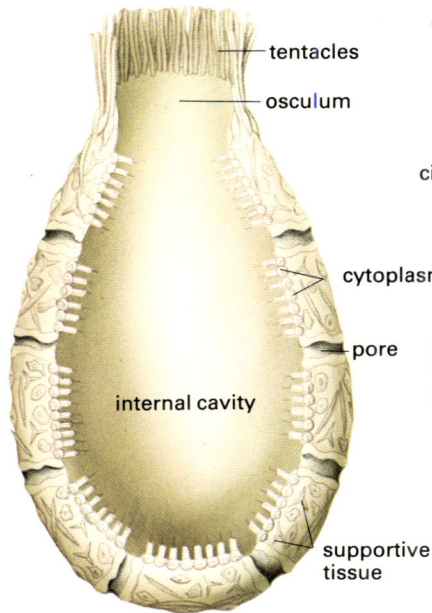

Sponge diagram labels: tentacles, osculum, cytoplasm, pore, internal cavity, supportive tissue

Sponge (primitive Metazoa)

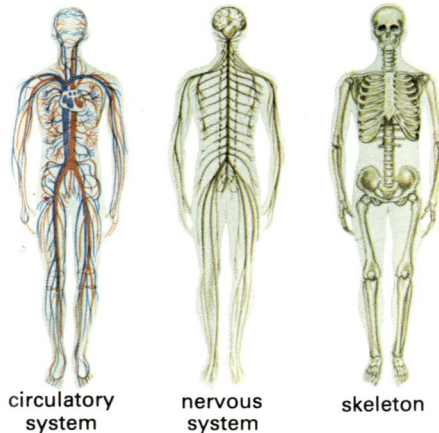

circulatory system   nervous system   skeleton

Man (evolved Metazoa)

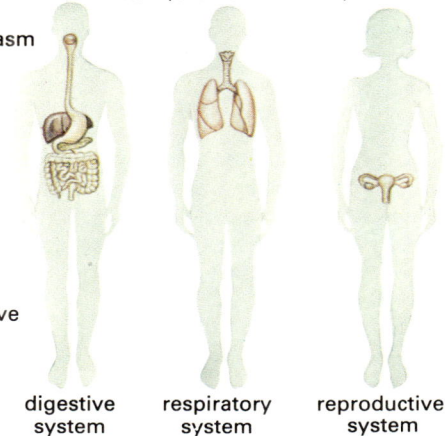

digestive system   respiratory system   reproductive system

Above, the three different levels of organisation which exist in animals. In the protozoan, the vital functions are carried out by a single cell, in a sponge by groups of specialised cells and in man, by numerous complex organs.

PORIFERS AND COELENTERATES

Sponges, as already mentioned, are called porifers because the walls of their cells are riddled with pores. What about coelenterates? This word derives from the Greek name that scientists gave to the single internal cavity of their body, *coelenteron*, meaning 'hollow intestine'. This single cavity is used for both digestion and the excretion of waste.

The Porifera and Coelenterata types each include three distinct classes, some representatives of which can be seen in the figure alongside. The sponges have hard material inside the body to give them strength. The two forms of Coelenterata, medusa and polyp, are shown in sketch form. Most Hydrozoa and Scyphozoa pass through both phases, but Anthozoa have no medusa phase, and spend their life as polyps.

All coelenterates are built on a circular pattern, with a central mouth which forms the only entrance to a very short gut. The mouth is usually surrounded by numerous tentacles which are armed with nematocysts (thread cells), some of which can inject powerful poisons which paralyse prey.

Below can be seen some spicules, the hard supportive tissues which are the skeletal elements of sponges, along with representatives of the three classes: Calcarea, Hexactinellida and Demospongiae.

A cutaway of a medusa and a polyp represents the two structural forms of Coelenterata, free-swimming and fixed, with examples of the three classes: Hydrozoa, Anthozoa and Scyphozoa.

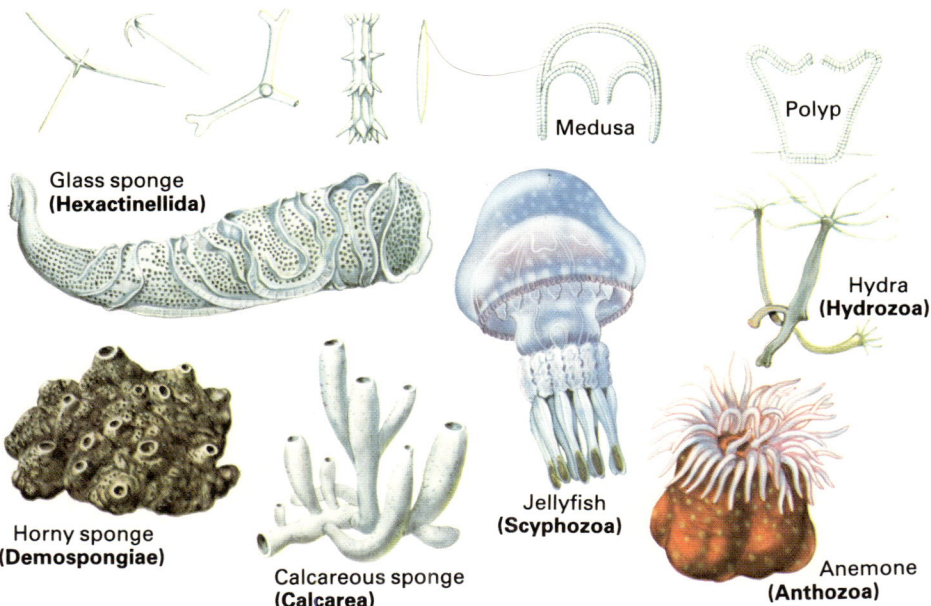

Medusa

Polyp

Glass sponge **(Hexactinellida)**

Horny sponge **(Demospongiae)**

Calcareous sponge **(Calcarea)**

Jellyfish **(Scyphozoa)**

Hydra **(Hydrozoa)**

Anemone **(Anthozoa)**

MARVELS OF ARCHITECTURE

A sack will not stay open and upright if there is nothing to support it. The same goes for a sponge which is a sort of living sack. Sponges need something to support them and many species of sponge have this support in the form of a skeleton. This skeleton is not a single structure but is formed by millions of tiny interwoven corpuscles called spicules, which form a supportive structure. According to the species, these are composed of mineral substances containing calcium or silicon. In other types of sponge, for instance the bath sponge, the skeleton of mineral supportive structures has been replaced by a network of bony substance formed by organic compounds.

How they feed

Not one drop of sea or fresh water is without microscopic algae or protozoa. When the water penetrates through the pores of the

Below: sponges drying in the sun on the coast of Cuba. All natural sponges used by man are bath sponges.

sponge and crosses the body, these micro-organisms are filtered out and provide the sponge with nutrition.

The sponge is able to eat this tiny suspended material due to the work of specialised cells covering the internal cavity of the body, the cytoplasm, which moves

Above: a large chalice-shaped sponge (centre of picture) photographed in the South China Sea.

rapidly. This movement causes a current which attracts the water towards the sponge and expels it through an opening called the osculum, after first having removed the nutritious elements.

Sponges are not the only animals that feed in this way. Bivalve molluscs and sea squirts all feed by this filter-feeding method.

SPONGES AND MAN

Nearly all the species of sponge used by man are commonly known as bath sponges. As previously mentioned, the skeleton of these porifers is not made up of mineral supportive substances but a thick network of bony substance called spongin.

When the animal dies its cells decompose and only the spongin framework remains, maintaining its original elasticity. Because of the spongin, this type of sponge is capable of absorbing and holding large quantities of water, and because of its elasticity, it can be used for a long time without losing its ability to absorb.

In the past, sponges had a lot more uses than merely being tools of the bathroom. In the Middle Ages, for instance, they were used for padding under the heavy armour of the knights.

The sponges that we use in our bathrooms are relatively expensive because they are hand-harvested. After harvesting, the sponges are dried, beaten and washed to remove hard debris, so that the only part remaining is the familiar fibrous, absorbent, spongin skeleton.

CORALS AND JELLYFISH
TWO STAGES OF EVOLUTION

The corals are part of the organised schemework common to Coelenterata (which also includes sea anemones and other plant-like animals). The coral is typical of the coelenterates and is shaped like an upside-down sack, with a mouth at the top and a certain number of tentacles. The lower part of the body is made up of a sort of peduncle, which the coral uses for gripping on to things. It lives fixed to the bottom of the seabed and, more rarely, on the bottom of lakes and rivers. The coral population belongs to the class Anthozoa in which there are corals that live singly and others which unite in colonies, often very large ones. Sea anemones also belong to the Anthozoa class.

In Coelenterata, where the mouth is pointed downwards and there is no peduncle, the animal is known as the jellyfish. Among the coelenterates, jellyfish belong to the class called Scyphozoa which is mostly comprised of jellyfish.

Living traps

Many coelenterates, such as the jellyfish, have a jelly-like body composed of over ninety-five per cent water. In spite of this, almost all coelenterates are fierce predators, or rather, living traps, although they do not 'hunt' their prey, nor do they capture it with tentacles, but sting and kill it with special stinging cells which shoot their poisonous liquid into the defenceless victim's body.

Once the prey has been stunned or killed, it is then drawn into the internal cavity of the body (the enteron) with the help of the tentacles that surround the mouth opening. Digestion is carried out in this cavity by juices produced by special cells. The nutritious elements are then distributed throughout the body while the undigested wastes are expelled.

Below: a sea anemone belonging to the genus Cerianthus. *Below right, a tropical madrepore, or coral, sometimes called 'brain coral' because its appearance resembles a brain.*

Above: the elegant shape of a eunicella, *an anthozoan which lives in colonies.*

Comb jellies

Comb jellies (Ctenophora) are a separate group somewhat like the jellyfish. Both have inner and outer layers separated by a jelly-like mass. The usual ctenophore is rounded, with a gastrovascular cavity opening from a mouth at the lower end. Ctenophores are hermaphrodites and shed their eggs and sperm into canals under the ciliary bands. Fertilisation takes place in the sea to yield a free-swimming larva.

Water Insects

Insects are by far the most numerous group of animals. There are over 750,000 different kinds of them – much more than all the other animal groups combined. They have been on earth more than 200 million years and have adapted to conditions in every part of the world, from the stifling heat of the tropics to the frozen wastes of the Arctic and Antarctic. They are found everywhere – on land, in the air and underwater. Some of them live all of their lives underwater, others on the surface film, and others are equally happy in or out of the water. Many of them are successful carnivores – sucking the body fluids of other animals for food.

1. Dragonfly (*Calopteryx virgo*): not a true water insect but spends most of its time flying around near the water. It is 48 mm long. Although it is not an aquatic animal, its larva, or nymph, is.
2. Larva of the dragonfly. Dragonfly larvae differ from all other insect larvae in that the labium is transformed into an extending forceps, by means of which prey is caught. The nymph creeps up the stem of water plants into the air to change into the adult stage.
3. Great silver beetle (*Hydrous piceus*): the largest of all the water scavenging beetles, and like all other water beetles it must surface for air. It breathes through its antennae.
4. Predacious diving beetle (*Acilus sulcatus*): found mainly in calm waters, but sometimes settles briefly in puddles in forests after heavy rainfall. It feeds off small aquatic larvae and crustaceans.
5. Common water beetle (*Haliplus lineaticollis*): common in ponds. It swims along by moving its legs alternately.
6. Water measurer (*Hydrometra stagnorum*): grows to a maximum of 10 mm long. It

is usually found on the surface of the water near the bank. Adult water measurers hibernate.

7. Water scorpion (*Nepa rubra*): the long tail is not a sting as is often thought, but a breathing tube with which the water scorpion penetrates the surface of the water to breathe. They do have a painful sting. They do not hunt for food, but rather lie in ambush and wait for tadpoles and small fish to come within reach, when they catch them in their front legs which have a jack-knife action.

8. Whirligig beetle (*Gyrinus substriatus*): small, shiny black beetles which gyrate in groups on the surface of stagnant or slow-moving waters. When alarmed they dive rapidly. They have two pairs of eyes, one for seeing above water and the other for use under the surface. They have strong legs that are well adapted for swimming.

9. Pond skater (*Gerris major*): is common on the surface of streams and pools. The male usually grows to around 14 mm long and the female is usually 2 or 3 mm longer.

10. Great diving beetle (*Dytiscus marginalis*): has to surface four or five times every hour to take a fresh supply of air into its air reservoir. It hunts diseased and weakened fish, attaching itself to a fish's back and sucking the food it needs from the unfortunate fish. It can go without food for up to one month and lives for about a year.

11. Lesser water boatman (*Corixa geoffroyi*): common in stagnant water. It feeds on small prey and can grow to 16 mm long.

12. Water boatman (*Notonecta glauca*): a powerful swimmer, usually swimming with its abdomen facing upwards. It can give a very painful bite.

13. Water cricket (*Velia rivulorum*): common on the surface of still and flowing waters.

14. Caddis fly (*Phryganea grandis*): not a true water insect but it does live the larval stage of its life under water.

15. Larva of the caddis fly.

16. Water stick insect (*Ranatra linearis*): 30–35 mm long and common near the shores of lakes and in ponds. It waits quite motionless amidst aquatic vegetation for prey. It lives for two years and hibernates. It lays its eggs in the stems of aquatic plants.

17. Saucer bug (*Naucoris cimicoides*): lives in slow-flowing water, ponds, marshes and puddles.

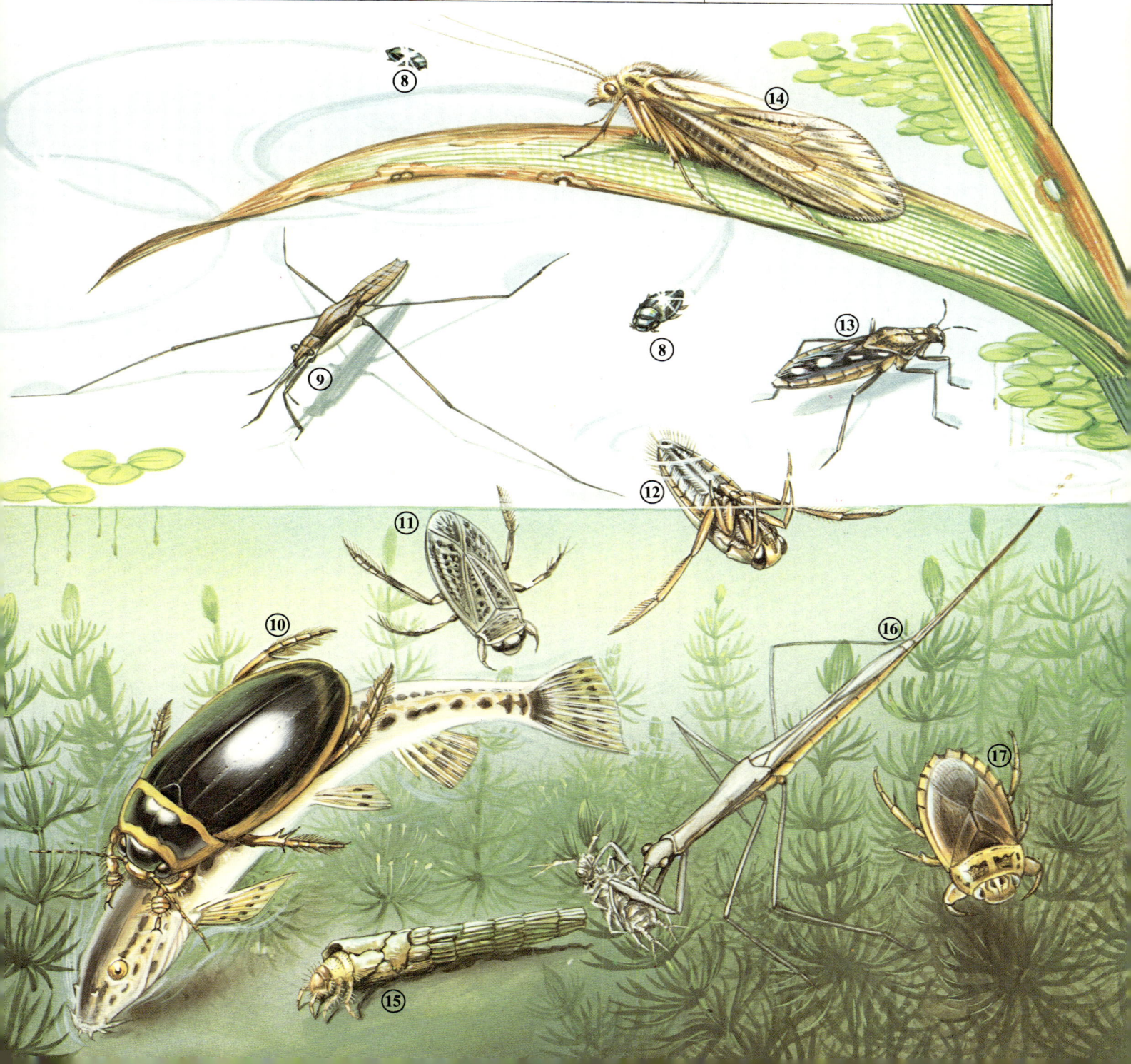

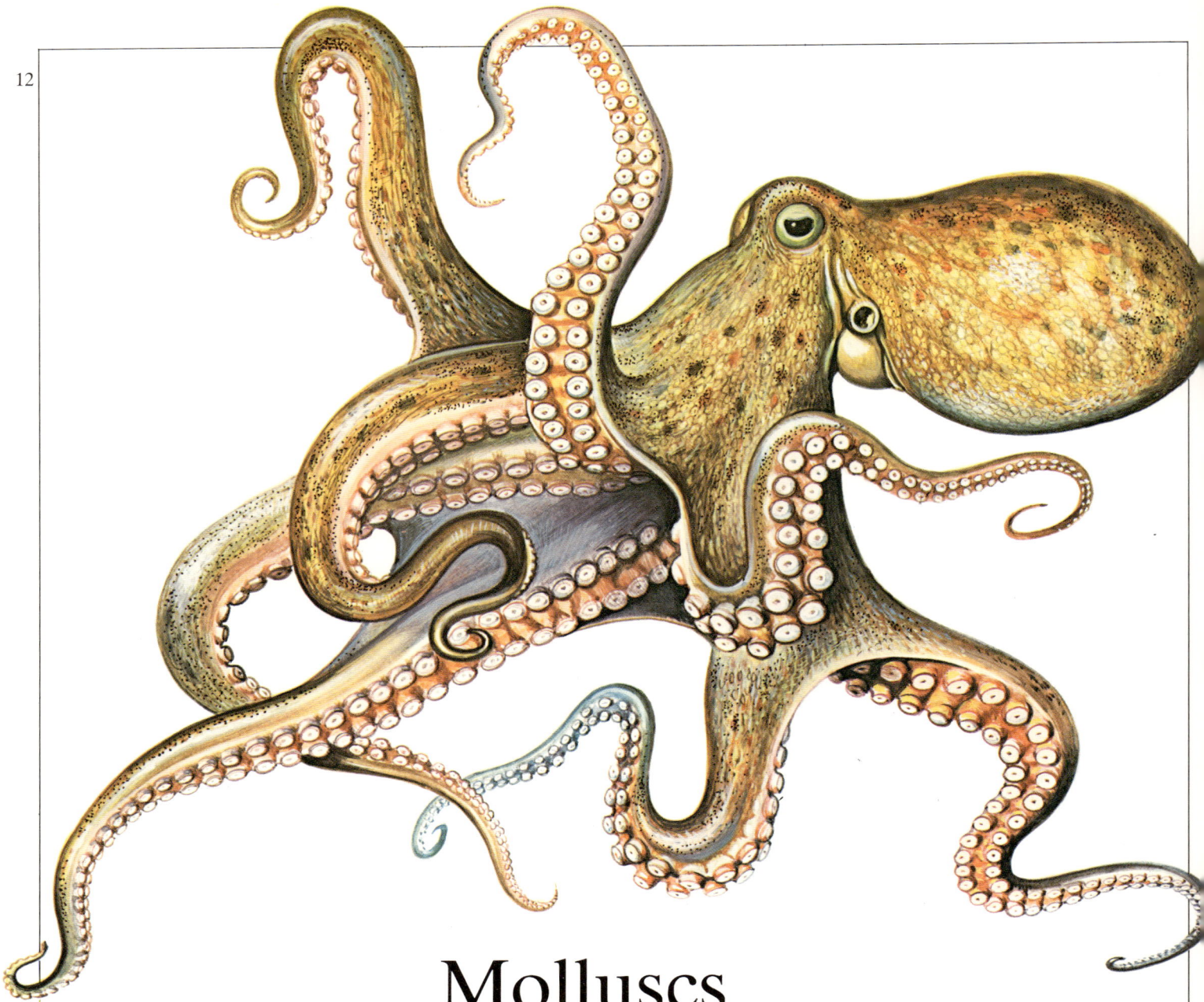

Molluscs

In an aquarium in Naples some lobsters were put in a tank alongside a large octopus. However, this was not a peaceful cohabitation. One after another the robust crustaceans disappeared into the mouth of the hungry mollusc. New lobsters were introduced and to avoid them being devoured too, a cement barrier was built. This proved to be a useless precaution because the octopus was quick to learn and climbed over the obstacle to continue its dinner. The phylum of molluscs is one of the most varied in the whole animal kingdom and one of the most interesting. There is no such thing as a standard mollusc form and classification can be confusing.

THE MOST INTELLIGENT OF THE INVERTEBRATES

The brain of the octopus is made up of 300 million cells. If we compare the proportions of this mollusc with that of man, this is a very considerable amount (in man the central nervous system is made up of around 10 billion cells).

Experiments carried out in laboratories have shown that octopuses have better learning facilities than other invertebrates. For example, in just six 'lessons', an octopus – which instinctively attacks crabs – learned not to touch crabs marked with a white cross because when it did, it was punished with a slight electric shock.

The octopus's brain is made up of several masses of nervous tissue which encircle the oesophagus directly behind the eyes. In other, lower, invertebrates, the ganglia are spread throughout the body, not centralised as they are in the octopus.

AN ANCIENT GROUP

The octopus, with its surprising ability to learn, is the result of an evolutionary process which began in remote prehistoric times. In fact molluscs appeared on the earth more than 500 million years ago, at the beginning of the Ordovician Period.

The evolutionary history of this group is very well known to us because most molluscs have always possessed a sort of protective skeleton which can be preserved in excellent condition as fossils for millions and millions of years – the shell. Every detail of their structure can be seen, even in shells which are hundreds of millions of years old, and shells which have been fossilised for merely a few million years are sometimes so well preserved that they are mistaken for modern specimens!

Molluscs increased in numbers and diversity as the years passed, producing species after species at an amazing rate.

CHARACTERISTICS OF MOLLUSCS

The snail, another well-known species, gives a good idea of the structure of molluscs.

The shell and the mantle

The snail, like many other molluscs, has a spiral-shaped shell (formed by a spiral which grows around a central axis). In other molluscs the shell is not spiral or helical, but formed by two shells hinged together, or is internal. Very few species have no shell at all. However, in all species that *do* have a shell, this is formed bit by bit by glands which are spread over a large part of the body surface. This 'skin' is called the mantle and is found under the shell. The shell is made up of a very fine layer of organic substances which contain a large quantity of calcium carbonate (chalk). On the sides of the body (or in some molluscs underneath the body) the mantle covers an indentation called the mantle cavity (or pallium cavity). In aquatic molluscs, this cavity usually contains the gills, the end of the intestine, the excretory organs and the genital tubes.

Snails have proved particularly adept at exploiting new habitats, both aquatic and terrestrial. The shell gives the advantage of protection, but it also restricts movement. As a result, some of the land and sea slugs evolved a reduced shell and some lost it altogether.

Land snails have many ways of coping with the most demanding environments. One such way is the epiphragm – a covering of hardened mucus which forms a seal in the aperture of the shell. When conditions become unfavourable, the snails form these epiphragms and become dormant. In winter this is known as hibernation. In hot conditions, the snail enters a state of aestivation which can last for months – even years.

Below: a species of land-dwelling snail common in Europe belonging to the genus Helix.

Above: the foot of the limpet in the photograph allows this mollusc to attach itself to rocks with a force equal to 15 kilogrammes in weight.

The foot

The snail moves by waves of muscular activity passing forwards along the body with the help of its most powerful member – the foot. The length of the animal's body is pushed along in this way.

In some species of bivalve (having two shells hinged together), the foot looks like a small finger which is pressed against the seabed and allows the mollusc to jump forwards, while in the octopus it is modified to form the tentacles.

The internal organs

The part of a snail that we cannot see because it is inside the shell is called the 'viscus sac'. It contains the largest internal organs, the reproductive apparatus, the heart, the intestines and the large digestive gland which could be compared with the liver of large animals. The oldest ancestors of the snail did not have a spiral shell and their internal organs were fairly symmetrical. With progressive spiralisation of the shell (the evolutionary process which took place over millions of years), the internal organs gradually 'rolled up' and lost their primitive symmetry.

Teeth on the tongue

The snail and other molluscs of the Gastropoda class have a single chewing organ, which could be compared to a tongue covered with tiny teeth, the surface of which would be something like a file. This is called the radula. Other molluscs, like the octopus, break up their food with a stronger organ similar to a bird's beak while others, like the bivalves, filter water and trap the micro-organisms contained in it. Some of these organisms are the bacteria which cause some infectious diseases which can be caught by people eating raw or badly cooked bivalves.

Where are they?

The most notable feature of this diverse group of animals is that its members are found in almost every environment on Earth – living in the world's highest mountains and the deepest floor of the ocean.

The animals shown below have not been drawn in proportion. The giant squid (22), an abyssal mollusc, can grow to a length of about 20 metres, whereas mussels (1), are just a few centimetres long.

Some of the best known marine molluscs are shown here. Number 1 to number 16 show the species which live on the seabed, either moving about it or actually fixed to it (the benthos species).

1. Mussels (*Mytilus edulis*): a favourite food of man.
2. Worm shells (*Serpulorbis sp.*): are gastropods with a unique bent shell.
3. Cowrie (*Cypraea tigris*): has a very smooth, shiny shell.

4. Lithodomes (*Lithophaga lithophaga*): bivalves which live in a cavity that they dig for themselves out of the rocks using an acidic secretion.
5. Sea hare (*Aplysia punctata*): looks similar to both a slug and a snail.
6. Tusk shell (*Dentalium elephantinium*): a typical representative of the Scaphopoda class.
7. Triton (*Charonia tritonis*): the largest of all Mediterreanean gastropods. The shells of some tropical species are still used as trumpets for sounding signals.
8. Scallop (*Pecten maximus*): a common bivalve usually found on sandy bottoms.

GIGLIOLI '81

Except for file-shells, it is the only bivalve that swims.

9. Mud file (*Lima inflata*): the mantle of which has long thin appendages.

10. Razor shell (*Ensis siliqua*): bivalve which lives almost completely under the sand.

11. Solenogaster (*Neomenia sp.*): a worm-like mollusc entwined around algae.

12. Octopus (*Octopus vulgaris*): a well-known mollusc which is frequently found in coastal waters.

13. Sacogloss (*Lobiger veridis*): green sea snail belonging to the genus Lobiger, *the body of which has algae-like appendages.*

14. Chiton (*Acanthoitona crinitus*): the best representative of the Amphineura class.

15. Fin (*Pinna nobilis*): the largest of all the bivalves found in the Mediterranean.

16. Torch mollusc (*Facelina coronata*): an elegant species belonging to the order of Nudibranchia.

The following molluscs do not attach themselves to objects and are free moving in the water.

17. Hyentine (*Lanthina janthina*): floats due to a number of bubbles wrapped inside a mucus net.

18. Argonaut (*Argonauta argo*): the strange shell traps air and gives buoyancy to it.

19. Nautilus (*Nautilus pompylius*): a cephalopod with a shell.

20. Cuttlefish (*Sepia officinalis*): has very large eyes and is a master of camouflage.

21. Common squid (*Loligo vulgaris*): has an exceptionally large brain.

22. Giant squid (*Architeuphis monachus*): lives in the marine abysses and can reach a length of up to 20 metres.

23. Vampire squid (*V. infernalis*): also lives in the deeps. It has a wide membrane held tight between its long tentacles.

WHERE THEY LIVE

Molluscs can be found in any area of the world – from mountain summits to the darkest marine abysses, from shallow shores to tropical forests – even in deserts.

In the sea

Representatives of all seven classes of mollusc can be found in the sea, while only two can be found elsewhere. There are marine molluscs which live stuck to the seabed. Others can swim freely about and others are carried along by the current. Among deep sea species are the largest of all invertebrates; the giant squids, which can reach 20 metres in length and, according to some people, even more.

In fresh water

Some species of Gastropoda live in fresh water and they are related to snails; such as the limnaeids which eat algae, and bivalves such as mussels which live partially buried in the slime, eating microscopic organisms.

On dry land

All land species belong to the class of Gastropoda and are usually called snails (when they have a shell) and slugs (when they are without shells). These animals live in humid

Among marine molluscs the most brightly coloured belong to the group of Nudibranches like this Coryphella verrucosa.

places, although there are some rare exceptions which can live in arid environments and even in deserts. To protect themselves from dryness, many snails withdraw into

their shells and secrete a slime by the collar. The slime dries to form a membrane which seals the opening but allows the snail to breathe. Sometimes the slime is used to 'stick' the snail to a flat surface. A few land snails live within the Arctic Circle, hibernating for most of the year, only waking up for the short Arctic summers when the temperatures rise barely above zero.

CLASSIFICATION

There are more than 100,000 species of mollusc which are divided by zoologists into the following six classes and one sub-class:

Monoplacophora

This contains two marine species. The *Neopilina* is one, the body of which has preserved its primitive symmetry, unlike other molluscs which have evolved beyond this.

neopilina

Amphineura

These are often referred to by their family name of Chitonida. Their bodies are protected by a shell made of eight plates. They live in the sea.

chiton

Aplacophora

This is a subclass of Amphineura. The animals in this sub-class have no shell and look like short worms. They live in coastal waters of tropical seas.

solenacea

Gastropoda

This is the largest of all mollusc classes and contains land, sea and freshwater species. Most species have a single spiral shell although quite a few land and marine gastropods do not have one. Most land species prefer to live in damp environments and secrete fluids to stop them from drying out.

snail

Scaphopoda

These are also called tusked or toothed molluscs because their shells, although tiny, resemble elephants' tusks. They live only in the sea and their bodies have tiny filaments.

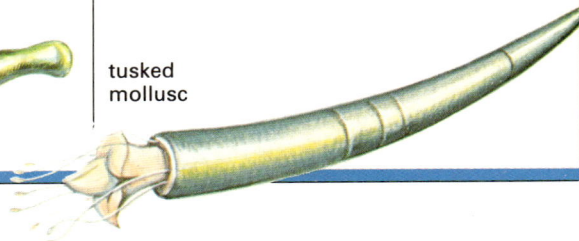

tusked mollusc

Bivalvia

They are called bivalves because their shells are formed by two valves which close and protect the body. They are the second largest class of mollusc and live both on the seabed and in fresh water. Their shells are hinged and can be opened and closed by muscle action.

clam

Cephalopoda

All species of this class live in the sea and have tentacles around their mouths. All modern species with a few exceptions (including the nautilus) do not have an external shell.

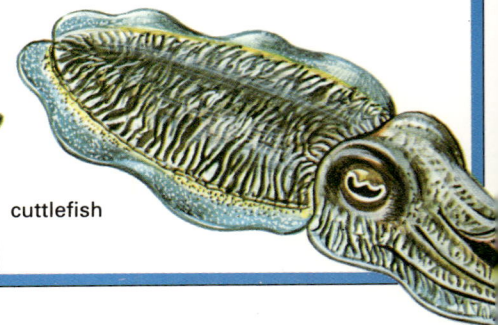

cuttlefish

Shellfish

Among the coral rocks can be seen a large, bright blue creature. Despite its considerable size, it looks very delicate. However, this is not the case. This animal, the giant clam (Tridacna) has, in its gigantic shell, the strongest armour existing in the animal kingdom. This shell gives the giant clam superb protection from its predators; the clam itself is completely harmless.

A SOLID
EXTERNAL STRUCTURE

Molluscs, or shellfish, usually have a soft body. However, in most species the body is largely, or entirely, protected by a strong external structure which is the shell. The protective shell, which is not a proper skeleton, varies greatly in formation according to the type of shellfish, and is mostly composed of calcium carbonate (over ninety per cent). This is the same mineral compound which makes up marble and calcareous rock.

More than 80,000 species of molluscs have been identified and named, making them the second largest group after the arthropods. They are grouped into six or seven classes; some scientists include the deep-sea burrowing forms in this group, others do not.

Propeller and bivalvular shellfish

Although there are many differently-shaped shellfish, there are basically two main types. The first type has an elongated spiral shell (propeller-shaped) which is typical of the class Gastropoda. The other type has two shells hinged together. These are the Lamellibranchia shellfish and are more commonly called bivalves.

In the illustration below are two examples of these shellfish showing their most important parts. Other shellfish have shapes that include blades (Chitonida), or a shape like an elephant's tusk (Scaphopoda). See the previous chapter for examples.

The attraction of shells

Because of their beauty, shellfish have, since ancient times, aroused great interest in man. Among primitive peoples shells are often used to make necklaces or as money, and one type, the money cowrie (see Group A number 5 on following page) was, until the last century, used as common currency in many tropical countries. Nowadays, shells are sought by man mainly for collections.

One particularly attractive shell, the Venus comb murex of the Pacific, is related to a tropical species that produces the dye Tyrian purple, much used to colour cloth in the past.

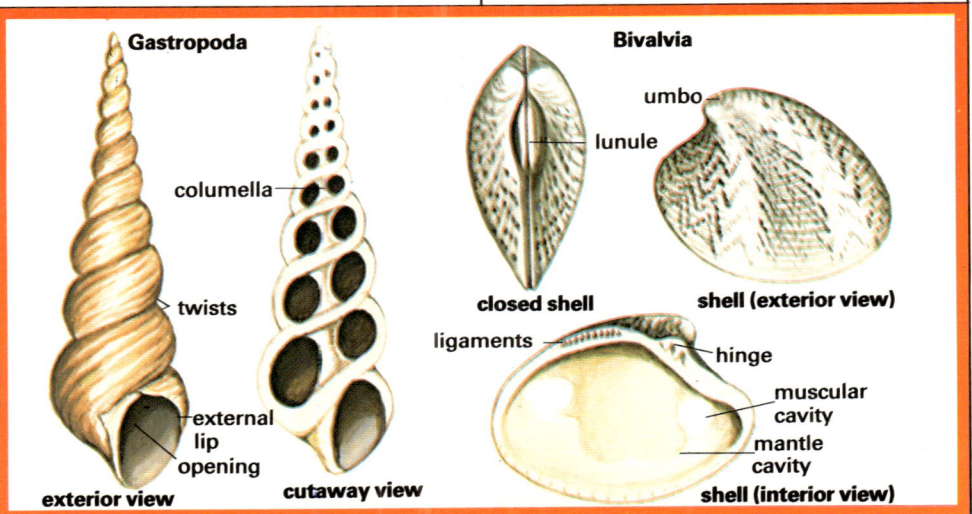

Gastropoda

columella

twists

external lip

opening

exterior view

cutaway view

Bivalvia

umbo

lunule

closed shell

shell (exterior view)

ligaments

hinge

muscular cavity

mantle cavity

shell (interior view)

*Shown in this illustration are some of the most beautiful shellfish. These are sub-divided into groups according to their classification. In boxes from **A** to **F** are shown the species of the Gastropoda class which are the most highly sought after by collectors. In boxes **G** and **H** are some species of Bivalvia. The environment of every species is indicated as well as the maximum length.*

A. Cypraea family: *This family is made up mostly of porcelains, which are probably the most beautiful and highly sought after of all because of their smooth shiny shells.*
1. Cypraea tigris: *Indo-Pacific, 12 cm.*

2. Cypraea aurantium: *Pacific, 14 cm.*
3. Cypraea mauritania: *Indo-Pacific, 11 cm.*
4. Cypraea mappa: *Indo-Pacific, 9 cm.*
5. Cypraea moneta: *Indo-Pacific, 4 cm.*
6. Jenneria pustulata: *Central America, 2 cm.*

B. Muricidae family: *The best known representatives of this family are the murices, molluscs that were used in ancient times for their purple dye.*
7. Murex palmarosae: *Pacific, 12 cm.*
8. Murex pecten: *Pacific, 15 cm.*
9. Murex brandaris: *Mediterranean, 8 cm.*
10. Murex radix: *Americas, 15 cm.*

C. Conidae family: *These are commonly called cone shells because they are almost always conical in shape. This group is very rich in species (between 500 and 600) and sought after by collectors, although the gathering of them can be dangerous because they contain poison.*
11. Conus aulicus: *Indo-Pacific, 15 cm.*
12. Conus marmoreus: *Indo-Pacific, 14 cm.*
13. Conus genuanus: *Africa, 7 cm.*
14. Conus geographus: *Pacific, 11 cm.*
15. Conus gloriamaris: *Indonesia, 15 cm.*

D. Tonicella family: *This group contains several large species which unite in groups*

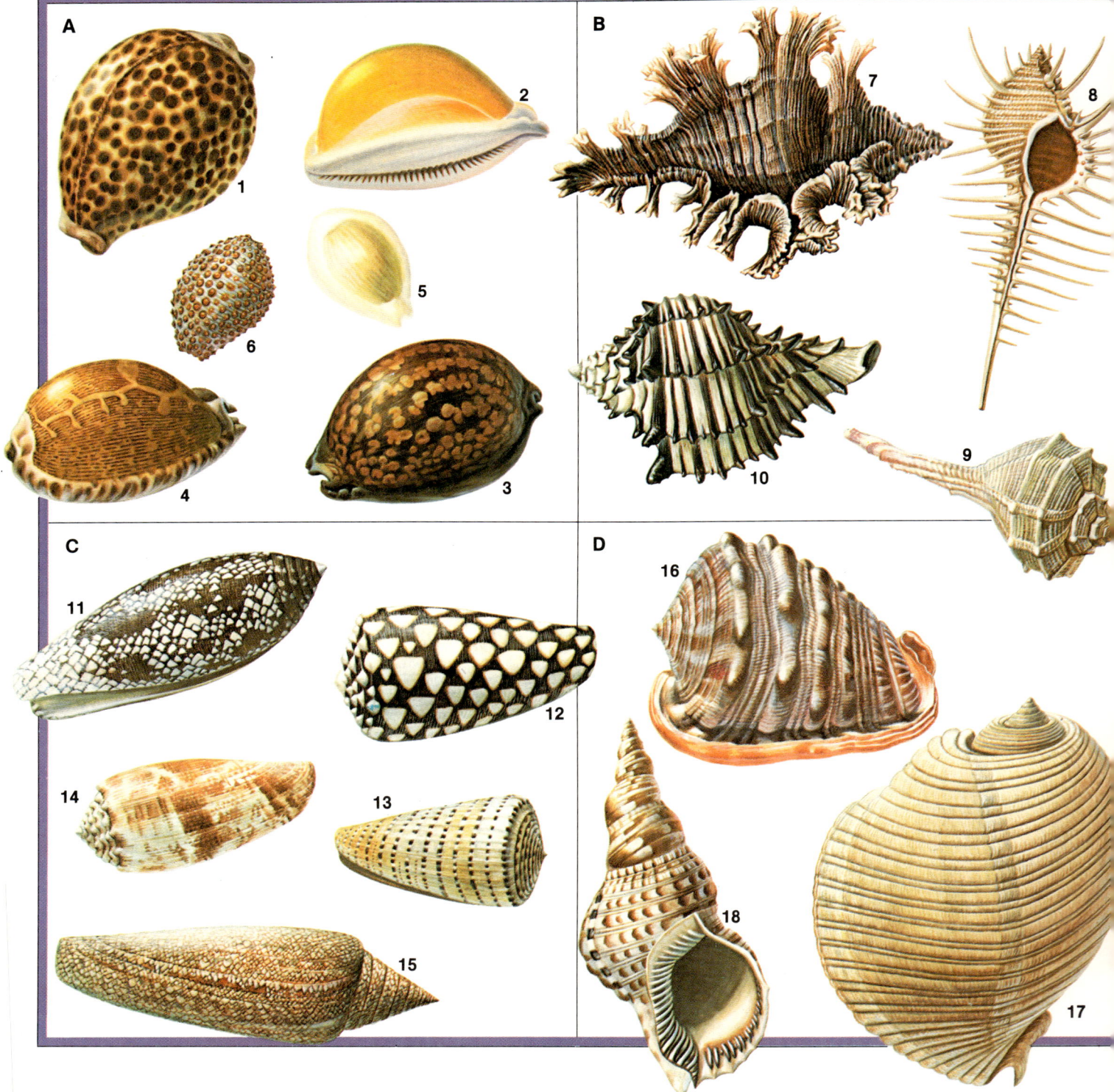

A
1
2
5
6
4
3

B
7
8
10
9

C
11
12
14
13
15

D
16
18
17

*that are often very varied within the family.
The two largest gastropods in the
Mediterranean belong to the Tonicella
family.*

16. Cypraecassis rufa: *Indo-Pacific, 15 cm.*
17. Tonna galea: *Mediterranean, 30 cm.*
18. Charonia tritonis: *Indo-Pacific, 45 cm.*

E. Volutidae family: *This family contains
short, spiral species and species with very
large openings. It also contains species with
elongated spirals and small openings. Some
of the shells in this group are prized for
their beauty.*

19. Harpa harpa: *Pacific, 7 cm.*
20. Mitra papalis: *Indo-Pacific, 12 cm.*

21. Melo amphora: *Pacific, 45 cm.*
22. Cymbiola imperialis: *Pacific, 25 cm.*

F. Strombidae family: *This family contains
a great variety of shellfish commonly called
conches or trumpet shells. They range in
size from under 2 cm. to 33 cm.* Strombus
goliath *is the largest.*
23. Xenophora crispa: *Mediterranean,
7 cm.*
24. Strombus latissimus: *Pacific, 21 cm.*
25. Lambis lambis: *Indo-Pacific, 14 cm.*

G. Pectinidae family: *These scallop shells
are perhaps the most beautiful of all the
bivalves and also the most sought after by
collectors.*

26. Pecten nodosus: *Caribbean, 15 cm.*
27. Pecten jacobaeus: *Mediterranean, 13 cm.*
28. Pecten nobilis: *Indo-Pacific, 15 cm.*
*This species varies greatly in colour. Below
are shown three different varieties of* Pecten
nobilis.

H. Tridacnidae family: *This is a small
family which nevertheless contains the
largest of all shells. This is called the giant
clam or* Tridacna *(shown below) which can
grow to over 1 metre in length and weigh a
quarter of a tonne. In spite of its size and the
many legends surrounding it, it is a totally
harmless species.*
29. Tridacna gigas: *Indo-Pacific, 130 cm.*

E

19
20
22
21

F

23
24
25

G

26
27
28

H

29

Crustaceans

In some European countries there is a phrase "to walk like a crayfish" which means to walk backwards. But do crayfish walk in this way? If so, why? What is a crayfish really like? It may seem peculiar, but crayfish, along with crabs and lobsters, belong to the same class of animals as the water flea and woodlouse!

HUNTER AND HUNTED

Crayfish usually walk forwards like all other animals. However, it is true that when they want to escape from danger they jump backwards, folding up their long segmented abdomen. When they are defending themselves they also move backwards. The reason for this is to keep their long, strong claws pointed towards their enemy at all times. The crayfish itself is, in fact, a formidable predator which is capable of attacking and killing all sorts of small aquatic animals but, at the same time, it is also a tasty morsel for many others, including man.

WHAT IS A CRAYFISH LIKE?

The crayfish is a freshwater crustacean. Like other crustaceans, it is well protected by a strong armour of numerous articulated segments, each of which has articulated appendages. This is a typical characteristic of the Crustacea which belong to the phylum Arthropoda.

To get a better idea of what the crustacean is like, imagine taking the crayfish apart, bit by bit, like stripping down an engine. At the front end it has two large eyes which are compound and stalked, and which allow it a wide view of its surroundings. It has a pair of small antennules which serve as smell and balance organs and a pair of long antennae which are used for touch.

The mouth is a narrow crack which is surrounded by appendages. On the thorax there are three pairs of appendages which are used when eating. Also on the thorax, the crayfish has a pair of stout pincers and four pairs of legs. The gills are folded under the body and protected by the carapace. The head and thorax are also protected by this. On the abdomen there are five pairs of legs used as swimmerets and for mating. The abdomen is formed of articulated segments. On the last segment are blade-like formations called the telson and the uropods which are used for fins when swimming.

The body of the crayfish is covered by a hard crust. As the crayfish grows it moults, replacing the old crust with a new one. The new crust is soft at first and then becomes encrusted by chiton and calcium carbonate.

The female crayfish carries her eggs in the underside of her abdomen. She lays them in mud and when the young hatch (usually in June or July) they are tiny and grow rapidly, moulting four or five times in the first year of their life. Crayfish, like all crustaceans, play a major role in aquatic food chains as the food for larger animals. The young crayfish are particularly vulnerable from other water animals. The adults are considered a delicacy by the greatest of all predators, man.

Above: a river crayfish, a crustacean which can reach 15 cm. Below: a 'dismantled' crayfish which gives a better idea of the various parts of its ectoskeleton.

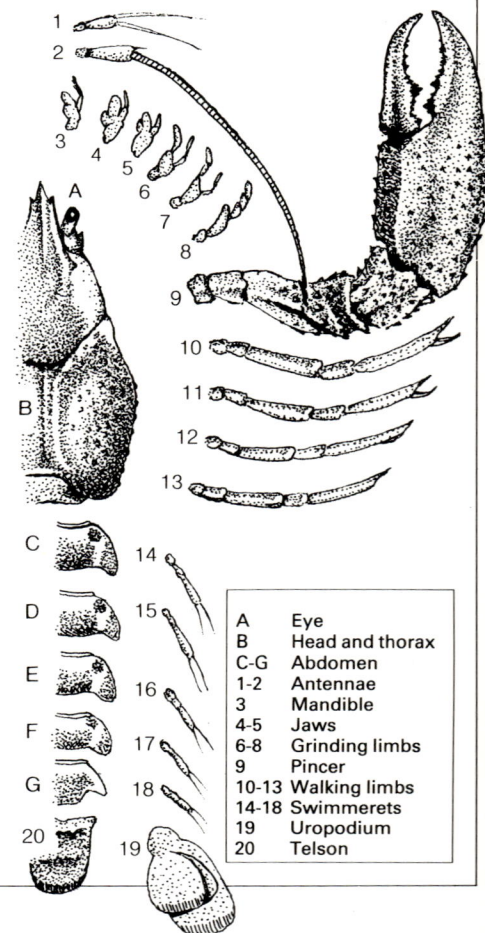

A	Eye
B	Head and thorax
C-G	Abdomen
1-2	Antennae
3	Mandible
4-5	Jaws
6-8	Grinding limbs
9	Pincer
10-13	Walking limbs
14-18	Swimmerets
19	Uropodium
20	Telson

DIFFERENT WAYS OF LIFE

The crayfish is a predator which hunts on the river bed and this type of behaviour is typical of many other species of crustaceans, such as crabs and lobsters which live in the sea. However, there are other crustaceans with totally different habits. Some species live stuck to the bottom of the seabed or on floating objects. Others are carried along by the current, while still others live on the water-line. There are also some parasitic species and species which have adapted to become land dwelling. The variety of ways in which crustaceans live is practically endless.

Stuck on the rocks

In tidal areas at certain times of the day the coast is covered (during high tide), while at other times it is dry (low tide). In this changing environment numerous barnacles live stuck on to the rocks. These are crustaceans of the sub-class Cirripedia.

What can be seen when the rocks are above water is a sort of tiny, light-coloured fortress which gives the barnacles their mollusc-like appearance. The 'fortress' is made up of five limy plates. Inside are the well-protected body and six pairs of forked filaments, or cirri (from which the subclass gets its name). The cirri are used to agitate the water, which helps the barnacle to draw in food. They are also used for respiration purposes.

Adult barnacles attach themselves to a support which they never leave. This is usually a rock or the hull of a ship, but a few attach themselves to other animals – such as whales!

Crabs and their houses

Hermit crabs are crustaceans with a soft and undefended abdomen. They almost always live inside abandoned sea snail shells. When the crab grows and the sea snail shell becomes too small, it is abandoned and the crab moves into another one. However, for some of them this protection is not sufficient, and they have devised other means of protecting themselves. Certain hermit crabs arm themselves by making their house sting to the touch. Everybody knows – and marine animals better than most – that certain sea anemones and jellyfish inflict a sting worse than stinging nettles and that it is dangerous to touch them. However, the hermit crab does not fear them. It pulls them off the seabed and puts them on its back. From then on they live together.

Some barnacles at low tide. When they are outside the water, these crustaceans close themselves completely inside their strong shells.

The hermit crab shown below (Pagurus arrosor), *lives in symbiosis with a species of sea anemone* (Calliactis parasitica) *which attaches itself to the shell that the crustacean has chosen as home.*

Besides the sea anemone, other marine animals also live in symbiosis with the hermit crab. Below is a hermit crab in symbiosis with a species of Hydrozoa (Hydractinia echinata).

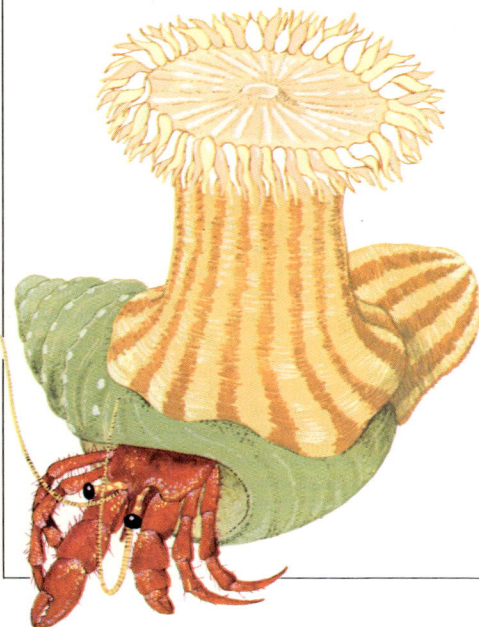

Above: a female planktonic copepod of the genus Cyclops, *with two large egg sacs attached to its abdomen. The name of this crustacean was inspired by the mythical Cyclops who had only one eye.*

Suspended in water

Plankton is the group of microscopic algae and animals (also usually very small) which live suspended in the water. In both sea and freshwater plankton, there are numerous crustaceans belonging to various subclasses, among which are the Branchiopoda, and, most of all, the Copepoda. These are mostly animals no more than a millimetre long; but there are some exceptions. In marine plankton there are some crustaceans a few centimetres long, like the *Euphausia superba*, little shrimps better known by their Norwegian name, *krill*. This name is best known to whale hunters because it is the main food of whales which swallow tonnes every day.

Crustaceans include about 45,000 species divided into eight sub-classes (Branchiopoda, Copepoda, Cirripedia, Malacostraca, Cephalocerida, Ostracoda, Mystacocarida and Branchicera).

Some of the best known crustaceans are illustrated here. The inset picture shows some of the smaller and larval crustaceans. Alongside each name is the sub-class.

1.   Goose barnacle (Cirripedia): *length from a few centimetres to half a metre. The body is supported by an adhesive sucker* and protected by a shell.

2.   Orniscus asellus (Malacostraca): *about half a centimetre long, this is the only species of crustacean to have adapted to a life on land. It can often be found on planks or trunks washed ashore and inside which it digs tunnels.*

3.   Dublin Bay prawn (Malacostraca): *up to 25 centimetres long, they live on the muddy bottom and are highly prized by man for their meat.*

4.   Corridor crab (Malacostraca): *a few* centimetres long, it lives on rocks and can even run outside the water.

5.   Lobster (Malacostraca): *measuring up to 50 centimetres, it lives on rocky coasts.*

6.   Swimming crab (Malacostraca): *up to 5 centimetres long, it lives in shallow waters.*

7.   Hermit crab (Malacostraca): *up to 10 centimetres long, it moves into the empty shells of other animals and lives on sandy bottoms.*

8.   Spiny lobster (Malacostraca): *this is the most highly prized species from a*

22

gastronomic point of view. Measuring up to 50 centimetres it lives on rocky bottoms.

9. Sea cicada (Malacostraca): *this species, which lives on muddy bottoms and measures up to 40 centimetres, has flat antennae which look rather like paddles.*

10. Telescope crab (Malacostraca): *up to 20 centimetres long, it lives on muddy bottoms and has singularly shaped forelegs.*

11. Small crab (Malacostraca): *up to 20 centimetres long, this crab, which has a spiny shell for camouflage, usually*

lives on a seabed rich in algae.

12. Crayfish (Malacostraca): *the only freshwater species shown in the large illustration, it is highly edible and lives in mud and under stones. It is 20 centimetres long.*

13. Cyclops (Copepoda): *about 1–3 millimetres long, they occur in both sea and freshwater plankton. The female carries eggs in sacs attached to the abdomen.*

14. Cyprid (Ostracoda): *drifts in the water until it finds a suitable place to settle. They*

are usually about one millimetre long.

15. Apus (Branchiopoda): *a few centimetres long, it lives in pools and swamps and sometimes even in puddles.*

16. Daphnia (Branchiopoda): *also called the water flea, this little species, only 4 millimetres in length, is common in pond water.*

17. Crysophelon (Branchiopoda): *this singular species, about 2 centimetres long, lives on the muddy bottoms of ponds.*

ODDITIES

There are many oddities in the world of crustaceans, as we can see when looking at the ones on this page. Crustaceans are a division of the phylum Arthropoda and the class contains about 35,000 species. Some of them are described below.

Changes during growth

Newly-born crustaceans, like insects, are very different from the adults. Growth does not carry on gradually but through metamorphoses (changes of shape). The initial larval form is called a *nauplius*. The nauplii are always microscopic beings and planktonic, with well developed legs and able to move very quickly. The following stages vary from group to group and have different names in different species. For example the larvae of the Phyllopoda type are very curious, as we can see from the larva of the sea cicada pictured below. The adult sea cicada is particularly strong and large and can be seen in the illustration on the previous page.

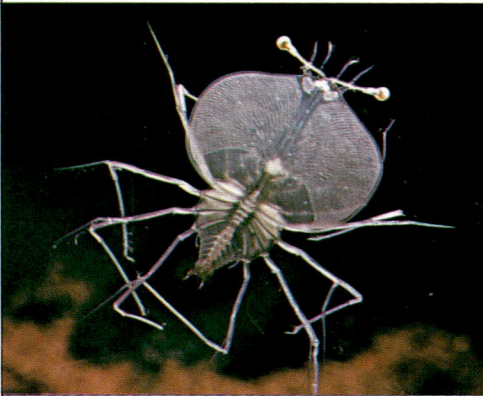

The two pictures above show a specimen of an Isopoda of the Ligia *species. On the left it is in a normal position, on the right it has rolled itself up into a ball in its characteristic defensive position.*

Below: A Sacculina *attached to the abdomen of a crab. It has roots which penetrate the entire body of the crab. It attaches itself to the crab when it is a larva and continues its growth fixed to its host.*

Armed fighters

The two crabs shown below are usually known by the name of fighter crabs. On tropical beaches the males of this species fight for the females using one of their strong pincers, which is exceptionally well-developed and suited for this purpose. One species of crab, the robber or coconut crab (*Birgus latro*), can climb trees!

Conquering dry land

Millions of years ago, some crustaceans left the water and became adapted to life on dry land: these are the *Oniscus* (woodlice) which belong to the order of Isopoda. They live in very humid places and live in cellars, underneath buried stones and rotting leaves and in damp bark. When they are disturbed, they roll themselves up into a ball. This way they present a hard, smooth dorsal armour which keeps them safe from enemies by protecting the legs, the antennae and the soft abdomen. A similar defence system is used by armadillos and for this reason, zoologists have named a species of *Oniscus* 'armadillidium'. The ability of woodlice to roll themselves up is not only used for defence purposes but it is also very useful in keeping them from drying out. The female carries her eggs in a broodpouch formed of overlapping plates which cover the underside of her thorax, and the young leave this as miniatures of the adult. *Oniscus* are found all over the world.

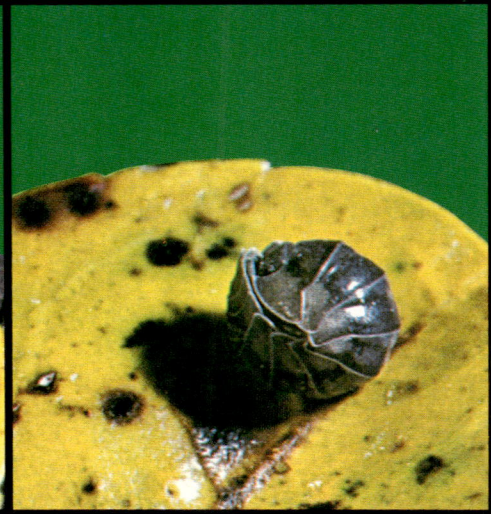

Shapeless parasites

What does the picture above show? It would appear to be a single crustacean but in reality it is two! If you look closely at the abdomen of the crab you will see a sort of shapeless sac which is a parasitic crustacean living on the crab, and because of the strange shape of its body, this unusual creature is known by the name of *Sacculina*. The *Sacculina* only attack other species of crustaceans and especially crabs. Due to their strange lifestyle, depending entirely on their host for nourishment, they have lost their external shell, their eyes, their antennae and all other appendages.

There are many other species of parasitic crustacean besides *Sacculina* which also have very strange body shapes.

TAKING IT EASY

Is it really necessary to describe the turtle? Their looks are unique among animals and impossible to mistake. They have armour which covers their bodies; they have blunt heads with toothless mouths; they have short, strong legs and very slow and calm movements. It is for this reason that people say 'as slow as a tortoise'. All the functions in the life of these animals are done at a very slow pace. If food is plentiful, they will eat. If food is scarce or lacking, they are in no hurry to find it. In fact, they can fast for a long period – as much as several months. Generally speaking, land dwelling tortoises are vegetarian, freshwater turtles are carnivores and sea turtles are omnivores.

As for dying, there is plenty of time for that too. As everyone knows, tortoises can live for a very long time and are perhaps the longest lived of all animals. But besides having a long lifespan, turtles are also ancient animals. Fossil remains of turtles date back over 200 million years. Since then they have changed very little in shape, and in an evolutionary sense they have progressed little.

Today, turtles and tortoises are widespread all over the world and are to be found everywhere except in Polar regions. They have adapted to a great many different environments and their habitats include rivers, swamps, woods, steppes, deserts and seas.

ANIMALS IN A BOX

Hermann's tortoise, a typical European garden tortoise, walks about the fields looking for tender wild salad leaves. If it is disturbed it immediately withdraws its head, legs and tail inside the shell, thus becoming an animal in a box. An American turtle, *Terrapina carolina*, is also known as the box turtle. The top part of its shell, called the shield, is very flat and the lower part, called the plate, is formed by three articulated sections. When this turtle withdraws into its shell, the plate is folded and sticks on to the shield, tightly closing the body in a solid and impenetrable box.

Contrary to what most people think, not all turtles are protected by a hard shell of horny plates. Some turtles have a soft 'shell' covered in a layer of leathery skin. In Asia these soft-shelled turtles are rigorously protected because of religious associations. Especially in Northern India, soft-shelled turtles are regarded as sacred and have been tamed sufficiently for them to take food from the hands of those who mind them.

The size of the turtles' eggs (they are always coloured white, regardless of species) varies according to species. The largest of the turtles, the Galapagos turtle, lays eggs that are 70 millimetres long and weigh more than 110 grammes.

Land turtles lay between three and ten eggs. Turtles which live in fresh water lay up to 40 eggs. (The turtles that live in the River Amazon lay up to 150.) Sea turtles lay anything from 50 to 200 eggs on the beaches that they visit once or twice a year. The eggs take from 70 to 270 days to incubate.

Turtles

In 1766, the French explorer Marion de Fresne captured a large specimen of giant turtle in the Seychelles. The animal spent the entire 19th century in the zoo, where it died, in 1918 after an accident, a good 152 years after it was captured – a really incredible record!

THE MOST ANCIENT REPTILES

Turtles are reptiles and, as already mentioned, very ancient animals. To appreciate this, one should think of the most famous dinosaurs such as the *Brontosaurus*, the *Tyrannosaurus* and the *Triceratops*, which appeared on the earth about a hundred million years after the first turtles.

Like other reptiles, turtles present the following characteristics:
1. They breathe with lungs.
2. They have a heart which is divided into atrium and ventricle.
3. They have a body temperature which depends on the temperature of the environment.
4. Their skin is reinforced by plates of bony scales.
5. They lay eggs which are able to develop in dry conditions.
6. Their skeleton is completely made up of bony tissue.

How they are made

The most obvious characteristic of turtles must be their external shell, more exactly called the carapace. The carapace is the part of the shell made up of bony plates. These vary in shape and size according to the species, but are almost always covered by corneous scales that can often be brightly coloured. The shell is made up of two distinct parts – a dorsal part called the shield and a ventral part called the plate.

In most turtles the shield is joined to the vertebrae, the ribs and the shoulder blade, except in the Dermochelyidae family, also called leathery turtles. These large turtles have a very special structure. In this family the plate is not joined to the internal bones, but is connected to the shield, rigidly in land dwelling species and in a more elastic way in aquatic species.

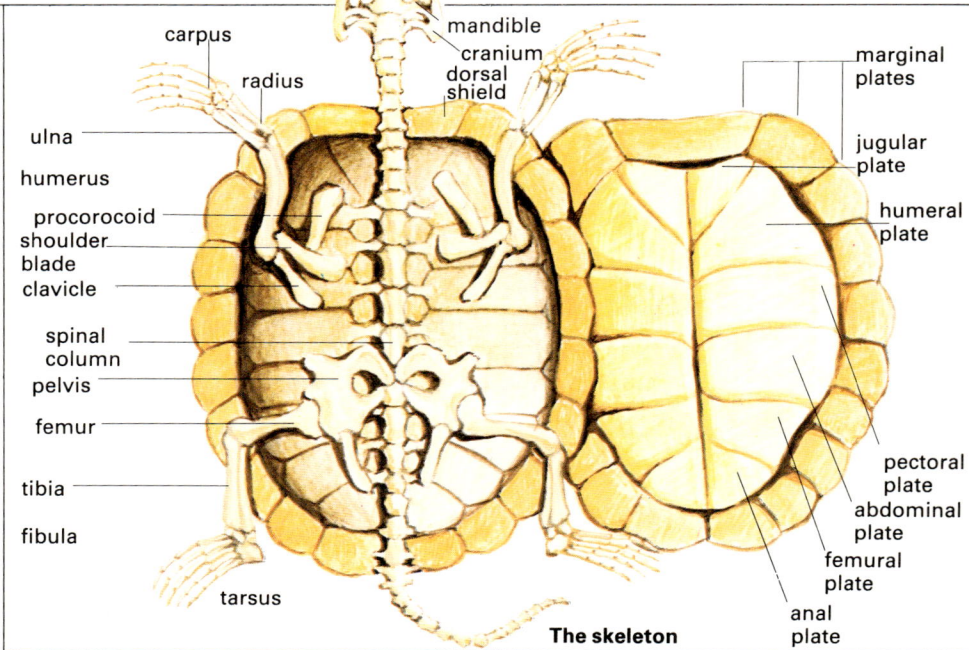

The skeleton

Labels: carpus, radius, ulna, humerus, procorocoid, shoulder blade, clavicle, spinal column, pelvis, femur, tibia, fibula, tarsus, mandible, cranium, dorsal shield, marginal plates, jugular plate, humeral plate, pectoral plate, abdominal plate, femural plate, anal plate

Because of the rigidity of the carapace, tortoises do not breathe with movements of the thorax. They inhale and exhale air from the lungs (which are extremely large) by a piston-like movement, i.e. by moving their head and other front limbs backwards and forwards.

Turtles' mouths are also unique in structure. They have no teeth and the jaws are covered by a bony layer which forms a sort of beak.

The legs of the sea turtle have become particularly efficient flippers which the turtle uses to propel itself through the water. These turtles only come to dry land to lay their eggs – up to 200 in a clutch. The huge, leathery sea turtle whose curious, degenerate shell is a mosaic of bones may weigh up to half a tonne. It feeds on jellyfish.

Above: On the left, the skeleton of a tortoise from the family of Emydidae, which is joined to the carapace (upper part of the shell). On the right is shown the empty shell of the same species viewed from below.

GIANT AND DWARF TURTLES

The smallest of all turtles are the mud turtles *(Kinosternida bauri)* which grow to up to ten centimetres when adult. The largest species is the *Dermochelys* (leathery turtle) which is a marine turtle that can reach more than two metres in length and can weigh over 800 kg. The elephant turtle of the Galapagos Islands *(Testudo elephantopus)* can weigh more than 200 kg and is the largest land dwelling species. Its shell can reach more than one metre in length.

DRAMATIC BIRTHS

The photograph on the left shows an enormous number of marine turtles on the shores of Ascension Island in the Atlantic Ocean. All the turtles are female and have come to lay their eggs on the beach. Every turtle finds a suitable place, digs a hole with its front legs and lays its eggs, which are then carefully covered. The eggs are warmed by the sun and develop in a few months. As soon as the young turtles break out of the shells, they have to embark on the most dangerous journey of their lives. As they rush towards the water, they are attacked and killed in enormous numbers by a great many predators, including mammals, other reptiles and birds – especially seagulls. Once they have reached the sea the males will never come ashore again. The females return only to lay their eggs.

CLASSIFICATION

Many people are of the opinion that all turtles look alike and that at most, there are two basic types – land dwelling tortoises and marine turtles. In fact, the order of Chelonia is widespread throughout the world with a wide variety of species which are quite different from each other. This is shown in the illustration on the right.

There are over two hundred species divided into two sub-orders and twelve families. The two sub-orders of Chelonia are Cryptodira which include the majority of the families and species, and Pleurodira which includes the families of Pelomedusidae and Chelidae. The two sub-orders were devised to differentiate between the structure of the vertebrae of the neck. The Cryptodires pull their heads into the shell with a backward movement, while the Pleurodires fold the head in sideways. The two largest families of this order, and the only ones found in Europe, each contain about eighty species. These are the Emydidae, which includes the numerous swamp dwelling species, and the Testudinidae, containing only land dwelling species, among which is the giant tortoise.

The green turtle is only partly or entirely herbivorous, feeding on zostera, the marine grass. Those that are partly herbivorous supplement their diet with molluscs or fish. The green turtle is also, unfortunately, the species that is used so much in the manufacture of turtle soup.

In the illustration on the right is a representative of ten of the families in the order Chelonia. Two of these, the leathery turtle or luth, and the big-headed turtle, are families with only a single species. The first is a rare, large marine turtle which lives in warm seas, and the second is found only in the fresh waters of the South China Sea.

TURTLES AND MAN

Turtle soup is a highly prized delicacy which few people have had the pleasure of tasting. It is made from the marine turtles which are caught when they come ashore to lay their eggs. Various other land and marine species are used by man for meat and eggs. The elephant turtles of the Galapagos Islands were hunted for centuries by passing sailors looking for fresh meat, and because of this merciless slaughter only a few specimens remain today.

Those that remain are now protected as an endangered species and there are severe penalties for anyone found attempting to kill them.

The bony covering of the shield of some turtles (especially marine species) is worked and made into various useful objects such as combs, jewellery boxes, and spectacle frames.

Chelydridae
Common snapping turtle
Chelydra serpentina

Platysternidae
Big-headed turtle
Platysternum megacephalum

Emydidae
European pond tortoise
Emys orbicularis

Testudinidae
Leopard tortoise
Testudo pardalis

Carettochelidae
New Guinea pitted-shelled turtle
Carettochelys insculpta

Trionychidae
Eastern soft-shelled turtle
Trionyx spiniferus

Pelomedusidae
South American river turtle
Podocnemis unifilis

Dermochelyidae
Leathery turtle
Dermochelys coriacea

Cheloniidae
Green turtle
Chelonia mydas

Chelidae
Australian snake-necked turtle
Chelodina longicollis

Amphibians

In the frozen wastes of Greenland, in the year 1932, some fossils dating back 350 million years were found. These animal remains were given *the scientific name of* Ichthyostega, *a name which in Greek means 'scaly fish'. These were not fish, but rather the oldest representative of the* *group of vertebrates which were the first to crawl out of the water and begin the conquest of dry land: amphibians.*

CONQUEST OF DRY LAND
Amphibians conquered dry land very slowly. The *Ichthyostega,* despite its strong legs, continued to live mainly in the water. Later, however, land-dwelling species appeared.

In full flourish
About 200 million years ago, the class of amphibians reached its highest point of development. Among the numerous species there were some very large ones, such as *Eryops,* an amphibian over two metres long. Like the crocodile, it lived near water and ambushed its prey, but it was also capable of living outside the water.

The development of reptiles
About 225 million years ago, there appeared the *Seymouria*. It was of modest size (total length of about 60 centimetres)

and had an amphibian's head while the rest of its body was unmistakably reptilian. It was a real puzzle for zoologists, who have yet to solve it. In any case, whether it was an amphibian about to transform itself into a reptile, or whether it was the first reptile to derive from an amphibian, the *Seymouria* represents a real link between the two classes. As reptiles began to spread over the earth they were the winners over amphibians in the competition for the conquest of dry land, and pushed amphibians back into the water.

Before that happened, the prehistoric amphibians had adapted well and quickly to the different conditions offered by the dry land. They were carnivorous, the smaller ones eating insects that were common in prehistoric coal forests and the larger ones eating fish or smaller amphibians.

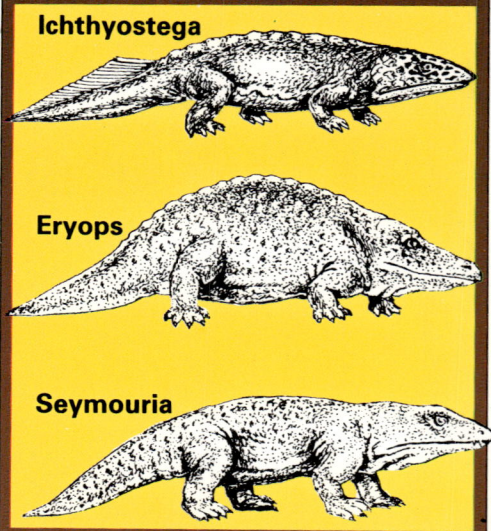

Ichthyostega

Eryops

Seymouria

ORDERS OF AMPHIBIA

The class of Amphibia contains a little over 2,500 species which are divided into three orders:

Anura (amphibians without tails). This group consists of about 2,000 species widespread all over the world but more especially in tropical regions. This order includes frogs and toads.

Urodela (amphibians with tails). This order contains about 450 species which live only in the Northern Hemisphere. It includes salamanders and newts.

Apoda (amphibians without any legs). They are from tropical regions and are like large worms, living mainly in the ground. They include a little over 150 species of caecilians.

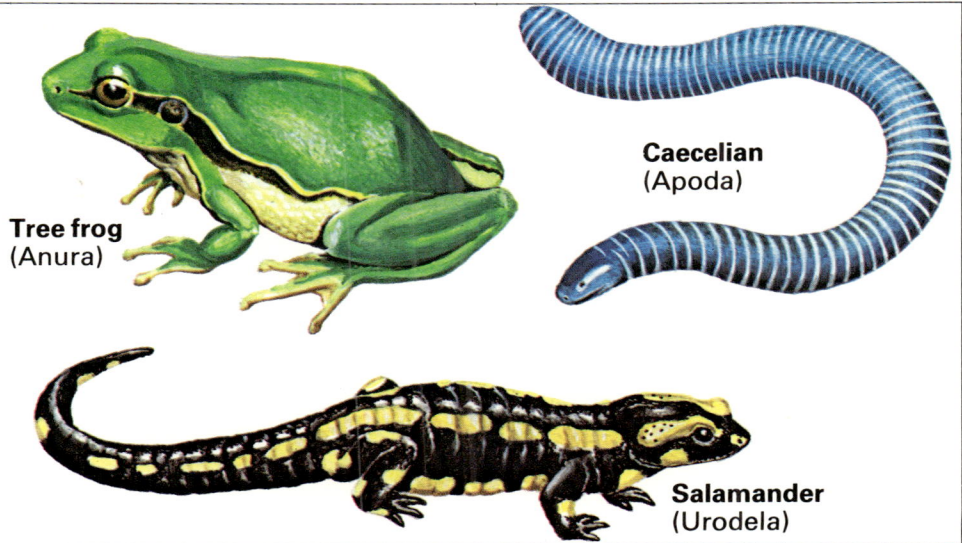

Tree frog (Anura)

Caecelian (Apoda)

Salamander (Urodela)

A CORRECT NAME

The word 'amphibian', from the Greek *amfi* meaning 'double', means having a double life. This is undoubtedly an appropriate name. In fact, in the case of amphibians, larvae and tadpoles live totally in the water, while adults often lead a terrestrial life, although even adults rarely move far from water or damp places for very long. However, there are exceptions. Some amphibians, such as the proteus, live always in the water and retain their gills throughout their lives.

The need for water

Almost all amphibians depend on water, at least during their larval development. In the series of illustrations below the main stages in the development of a frog can be seen, from egg to adult via the various intermediate stages of spawn and tadpoles (metamorphoses).

Liberation from the water

Some amphibians have succeeded in completely moving away from their aquatic environment. This is so in the case of the black salamander which lives in the Alps at about 3,000 metres. The female of this species, after a long gestatory period, gives birth to two to four young which already resemble

the adults. Therefore the metamorphosis takes place inside the body of the mother. Like the black salamander, caecilians have little need of water and they pass a large part of their lives on dry land. These animals, which look like worms, measure from a little over 5 centimetres up to 1.5 metres.

Odd breeders

Some frogs lay their eggs in pools of water held in branches of trees, or in the droplets of water found at leaf bases. The female Surinam toad carries the eggs embedded in her back, and metamorphosis takes place in the egg.

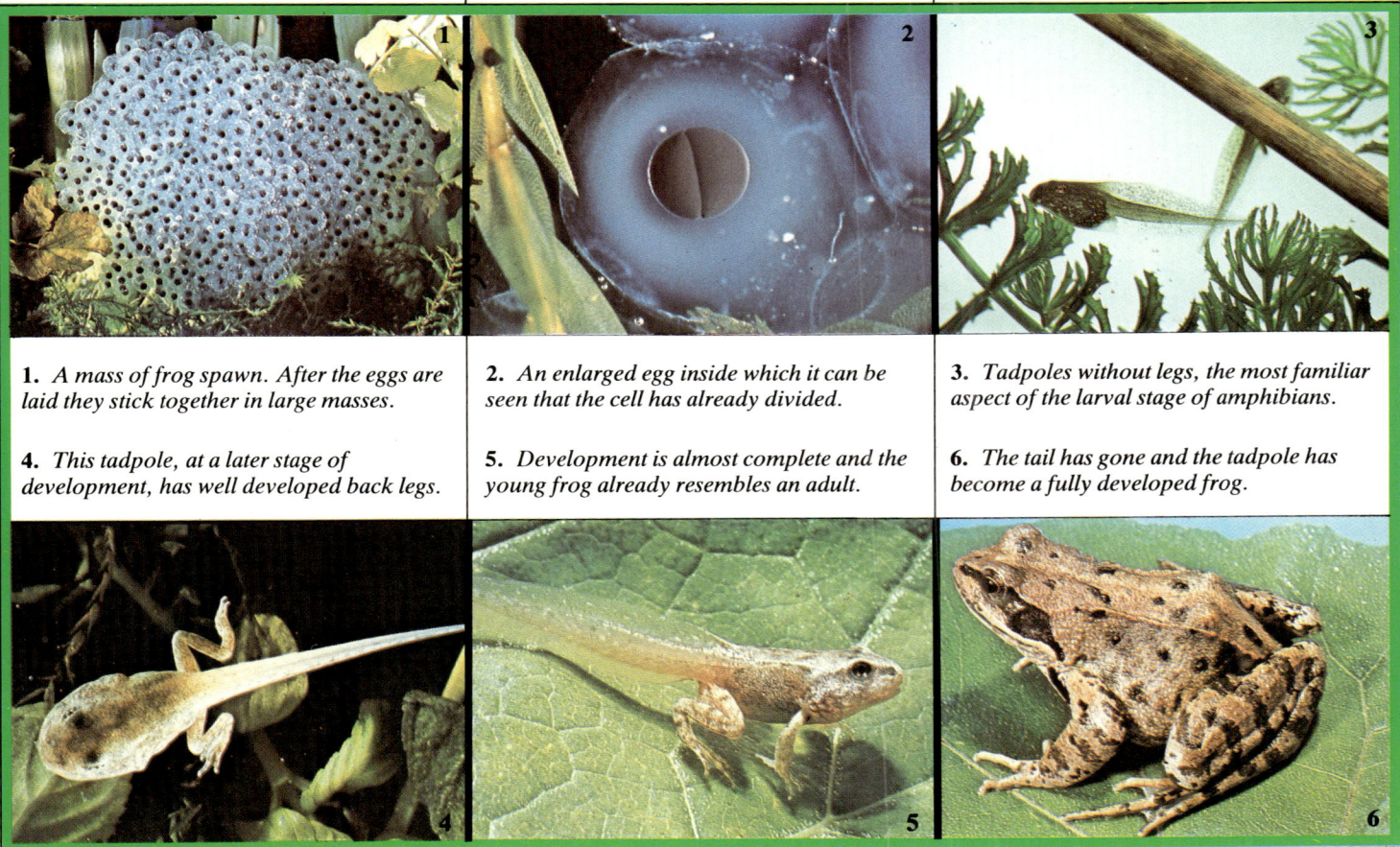

1. *A mass of frog spawn. After the eggs are laid they stick together in large masses.*

2. *An enlarged egg inside which it can be seen that the cell has already divided.*

3. *Tadpoles without legs, the most familiar aspect of the larval stage of amphibians.*

4. *This tadpole, at a later stage of development, has well developed back legs.*

5. *Development is almost complete and the young frog already resembles an adult.*

6. *The tail has gone and the tadpole has become a fully developed frog.*

Eardrum — Lungs (partly raised to show the heart) — Heart — Stomach — Cloaca — Liver — Bladder — Intestine

Shoulder blades — Ribs — Pelvis — Urostyle

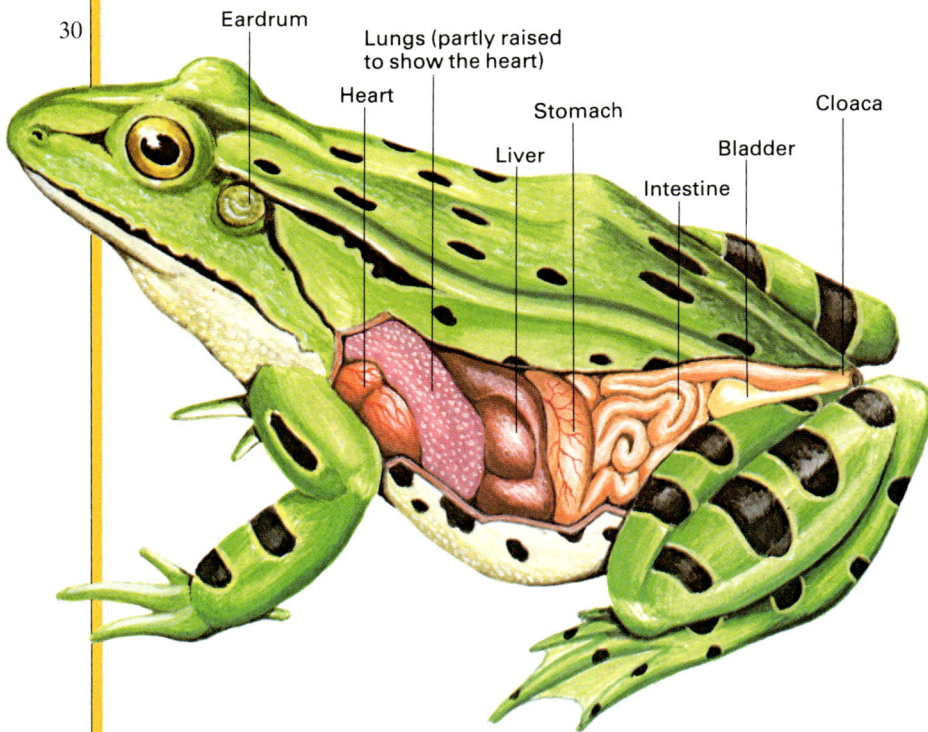

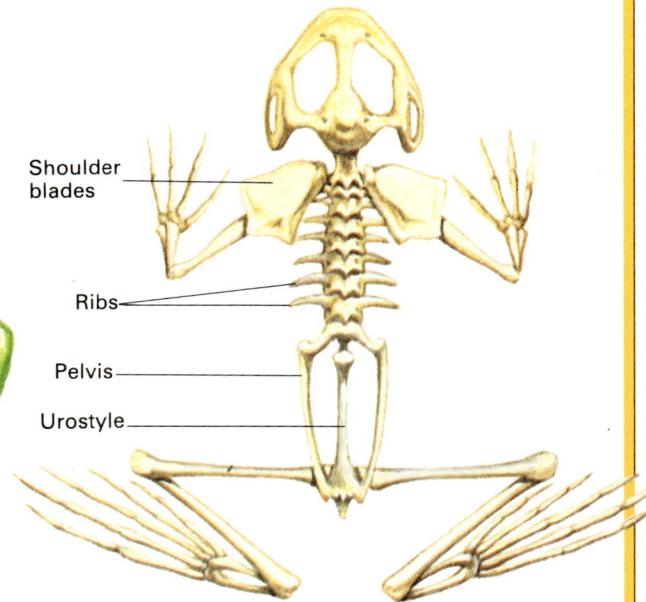

OBSERVING AN AMPHIBIAN
The frog (above) is typical of all amphibians in the following respects.

Eyes: Each eye is protected by two lids, the upper of which is short and fixed, and the lower which is transparent and covers the whole cornea.

Nostrils: Are situated at the front of the head and connect the olfactory (pertaining to smell) organ cavities with the outside.

Eardrum: The membrane of the eardrum is attached to the skin; in fact the external ear is not present.

Mouth: Usually has small, constantly growing teeth (without roots) supported by the jaw and the palate.

Tongue: In the Anura the tongue is very mobile. It is attached to the front of the mouth and can be shot out very quickly to catch small prey.

Vocal sac: Is present only in males. It puffs up when the frog 'croaks' and is used as a sound box for the noises made by the larynx. This is why the frog's croak is so 'throaty'.

Heart: Is partially divided into the right part (venous) and the left part (arterial). The right auricle is where blood from the veins arrives and is separated from the left auricle where blood from the artery arrives. There is only one ventricle, therefore the venous blood and the arterial blood mix and the organs of the body receive blood which is never perfectly oxygenated.

Lungs: These are very small. In amphibians, cutaneous respiration (through the skin) is more important than pulmonary (lung) respiration. They are always lacking in tadpoles, and in some species, even in adults.

Cloaca: This is a single aperture out of which the eggs or sperm make their exit, also urogenital (waste) material.

Bone structure: The spinal column is made up of only five to eight vertebrae and continues into the pelvis through the urostyle, a bony rod formed by the fusion of several vertebrae. The ribs are very short and are not joined to the sternum. The front limbs end in four toes. The back limbs fold into a 'Z' shape (in a special position which allows them to jump) and end in five toes.

A SKIN FOR ALL OCCASIONS
Amphibians have naked skin. That means that they are only protected on the surface by a thin corneous layer, which continually renews itself. It is rich in glands which create mucus to keep it damp and elastic. In amphibians the skin is an organ with many uses. All amphibians absorb the water they need through the skin and do not drink through the mouth. Moreover, oxygen from the air dissolves on the thin layer of mucus and is absorbed directly by the blood which circulates through the skin vessels. This cutaneous respiration accounts for from seventy to eighty per cent of the total needed by a frog. Some amphibians, such as toads, use their skin for defence. In these animals the skin has glands which contain poison. Although this is harmless to man, it discourages almost all possible predators from attacking it.

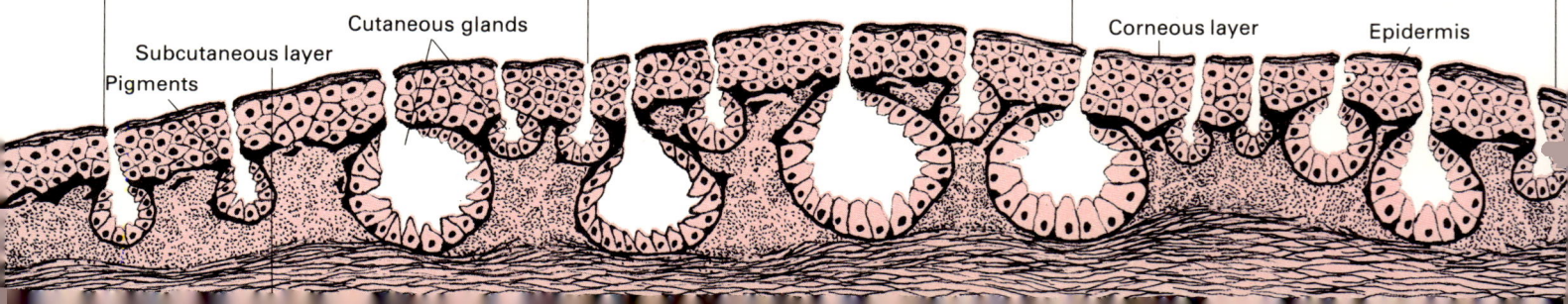

Pigments — Subcutaneous layer — Cutaneous glands — Corneous layer — Epidermis

WINTER OR SUMMER REST

Amphibians' blood is never perfectly oxygenated, as it is in birds and in mammals. Add to this type of circulation the fact that their respiration does not maintain a high level of muscular combustion, and the result is that the body temperature of amphibians, and also fish and reptiles, varies with that of the environment. Not being able to keep the body temperature constant means that their activity follows the rhythms of the seasons. During the winter they usually reduce their activity, almost going to sleep in warm sheltered places, always near water. This lethargic state in amphibians is not proper hibernation as with some mammals, such as hedgehogs. Any small rise in temperature is enough to revive them. Other species which live in areas with mild winters and hot, dry summers, rest at the opposite time of year, during the summer months. In this case it is called aestivation (summer rest).

EGG SWALLOWERS

The female of the Australian frog (*Rheobatrachus selus*) swallows the fertilised eggs which she has laid and keeps them in her throat until they hatch. The hatched tadpoles then move into their mother's stomach where their presence stops the digestive process. If the female is forced to disgorge the tadpoles they die, for they are not able to live in the water before metamorphosis. A variety of tree-frog, (*Hylambates*) keeps the fertilised eggs in her mouth until they hatch as adults.

AN ATTENTIVE FATHER

Most amphibians abandon their eggs after laying them, but there are some exceptions. The male midwife toad, an Anura which lives in Western Europe, gathers up the eggs and carries them about on its back legs. He is a very attentive father.

WIDESPREAD EVERYWHERE

Except in Polar regions (where no cold-blooded terrestrial animal could survive) and deserts, amphibians are found everywhere. Besides the numerous species which live in pools, there are amphibians which live in the vegetation and on the floor of tropical forests. Others live high in the mountains, while the caecilians spend most of the time underground.

Finally, some amphibians are adapted to life in totally dark places, such as caves, and in some cases they have become totally blind. On the following pages some of the best-known species of amphibian are illustrated.

A TADPOLE FOR EVER!

The tiger salamander (Ambystora tigrinium) is one of the most common American Urodela. It looks like a European spotted salamander but the tadpole, due to the cold or other causes, might never undergo metamorphosis, although it is sexually mature and able to reproduce at the larval stage.

This phenomenon is called 'neoteny'. At one time the neotenous form of the tiger salamander was considered a species in its own right and is still, today, often given its common ancient name 'axolotl', which is of Mexican origin.

In fact, in the past, the axolotl (a specimen of which can be seen below), was sought after by Central American peoples for its meat. In other species neoteny is not an exception, but the rule. This is so in the case of the proteus, an amphibian which lives exclusively in cave water and which keeps its gills all its life.

On this page we can see some of the best known species belonging to the order of Urodela. On the opposite page (10 onwards) are some of the best known species belonging to the order of Anura:

1. **Black salamander** (*Salamandra atra*).
2. **False newt** (*Pseudotriton montanus*).
3. **Tiger salamander** (*Ambystoma tigrinum*).
4. **Alpine newt** (*Triturus alpestris*).
5. **Violet salamander** (*Dicamptodon ensatus*).
6. **Mud-puppy** (*Necturus maculosus*).
7. **Japanese giant salamander** (*Andrias japonicus*).
8. **Crested newt** (*Triturus cristatus*).
9. **Amphiuma** (*Amphiuma means*).
10. **Firebelly toad** (*Bombina variegata*).
11. **Green frog** (*Rana esculenta*).
12. **Hairy frog** (*Trichobatrachus robustus*).
13. **Surinam toad** (*Pipa pipa*).
14. **Bell's frog** (*Ceratophrys dorsata*).
15. **Common toad** (*Bufo bufo*).
16. **Reed frog** (*Hyperolius viridiflavus*).
17. **Arrow-poison frog** (*Dendrobates typographicus*).
18. **White's tree frog** (*Hyla coerulea*).
19. **European spadefoot toad** (*Pelobates fuscus*).
20. **Mantella** (*Mantella aurantiaca*).
21. **Atelope** (*Atelopus varius*).
22. **Marine toad** (*Bufo marinus*).
23. **Horned frog** (*Megophrys monticola*).

In the inset are some of the cave amphibians belonging to the order of Urodela:
24. **Underground newt** (*Hydromantes italicus*).
25. **Proteus** (*Proteus anguineus*).
26. **Blind salamander** (*Typhlomolge rathbuni*).

E. GIGLIOLI '81

Life in the River

Imagine sailing along the River Nile. Here and there can be seen something immobile floating on the surface. Suddenly, with an enormous splash, two giant animals appear. Their unmistakable muzzles show immediately what they are – two hippopotamuses. Now the giants face up to each other, opening their huge mouths and trying to bite each other. This is a duel between males, no holds barred, probably the most terrifying spectacle to be seen in any river. Hippopotamuses live in lakes, rivers and swamps throughout Africa south of the Sahara. They come on to the land at night to feed and often cause considerable damage to local crops.

HORSES OF THE RIVER

The word hippopotamus means 'river horse' (from the Greek *hippos* meaning horse and *potamus* meaning river).

The hippo is a very large 'horse'. It can reach a weight of four tonnes, a length of four metres and a height of 1.5 metres. It has an enormous mouth and two huge lower canines which can measure more than 60 centimetres in height. The mighty tusks are not only used as weapons in battles between males, but also as tools for pulling up algae on which it feeds during the day.

In fact, the hippopotamus is exclusively vegetarian. During the day it eats algae and other aquatic plants, while at night it leaves the river and grazes on dry land. Although it eats enormous amounts of vegetation, this giant is also useful – the excrement which it deposits in the river helps to increase the fertility of the waters.

However, the hippopotamus is not the only animal to live in a river.

THE PROBLEMS OF A RIVER DWELLER

Like all other living beings, river dwellers have to tackle problems which can make their lives difficult. First there is the problem of the speed and strength of the currents. The temperature of the water and amount of oxygen in it depends on these two factors. Both are indispensable to the respiration of the animals and also account for the type of river bed. Currents, therefore, heavily influence both the environment and the living beings in it.

For example, mountain torrents are favourable to trout which are capable of living in roaring gorges. If there is no current, or very little, conditions will become similar to those of a pool or lake, where plankton (the enormous quantities of microscopic animal and plant organisms which live suspended in the water) is to be found. In fast flowing rivers there is no plankton, for it would be swept away by the current.

TYPES OF WATER

The water of a spring bubbles out of the rocks and is the beginning of a roaring mountain torrent. The water is very cold and clear. It is rich in oxygen, for the fast flow of the water continually mixes it with the air. It is also rich in mineral salts which were dissolved in it while the water was underground.

The temperature is higher on the plains and the water is correspondingly poorer in oxygen and more sluggish because of the large number of particles suspended in it.

At an estuary, the water of a river mixes with that of the sea and becomes more salty. However, the salinity depends on the size of the river and the tides.

River vegetation

Because of photosynthesis, organisms can transform inorganic substances into organic substances or 'living' matter.

Most important are the diatoms, the green, brown, blue and blue-green algae, microscopic plant organisms which are almost invisible to the naked eye. They constitute the main source of living matter in fresh water. Alongside these tiny organisms there are numerous superior (with leaves and roots) plants, some of which, like algae, live totally underwater.

Great travellers

Some river animals do not spend all their lives in the river, but move from rivers to the sea (or vice-versa) to carry out the various phases of their biological cycle. Salmon, hatched in mountain streams, move out to the sea where they remain until they

A salmon leaping up a waterfall to reach its spawning ground.

are sexually mature. They then return to the waters where they were born, to reproduce. In doing this, they undergo a long, tiring journey against the current.

An even longer journey is made by the eel. Born in the Sargasso Sea, the eel then crosses the Atlantic Ocean to reach European rivers where it continues to live. When it is ready to reproduce, it returns to its place of origin.

No part of the living space provided by a river is neglected. There are plants that root on the bottom and float on the surface. There are insects that burrow in the silt whose larvae are the food of newts and fish, which in turn are eaten by birds such as herons. A day spent nature-watching by a

river is an exciting and rewarding one.

River visitors

Many forms of life are continually entering a river. Some examples are leaves which fall off trees and insects which fall into the water. These innocent visitors are an important source of food for river-dwelling animals – the trout will even jump out of the water to catch an insect.

But there are also many which just as innocently depart. Rats, being the veritable skin divers that they are, prey on certain molluscs. The aquatic larvae of some insects, such as dragonflies, turn into adults which eventually abandon the river and take to the air.

Some animals leave the river, such as the mollusc, preyed on by the rat (a), another the dragonfly (b). Others enter, such as the butterfly which has fallen into the water (c).

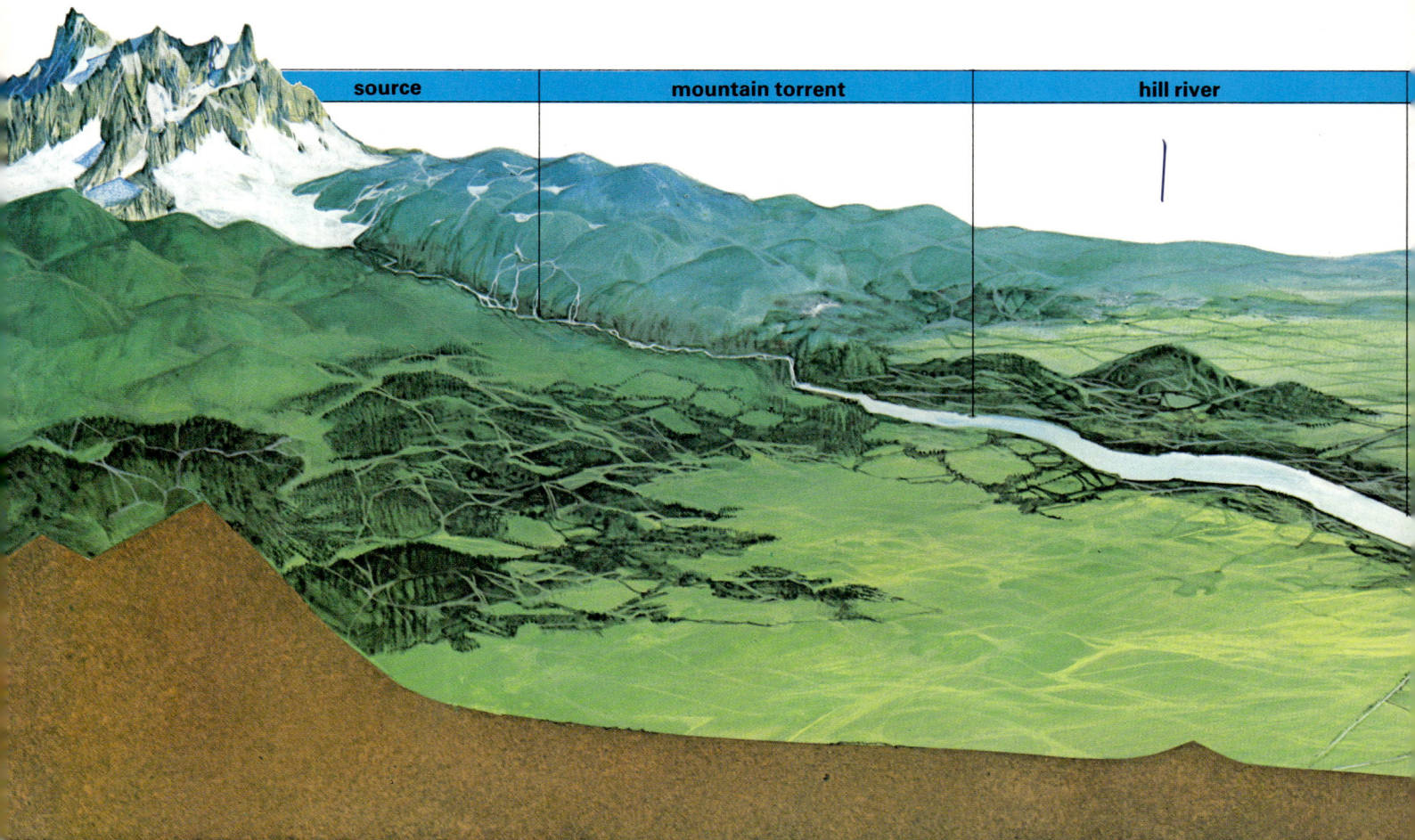

| source | mountain torrent | hill river |

rock

rocks and stones

stones and pebbles

A JOURNEY ALONG A LONG RIVER

Imagine going on a journey along a large European river. The river can be divided into various stages, each with a different type of environment.

The source

Here the current is very strong and the water, which bubbles out from the depths of the ground, does not suffer from changes in the seasons.

On the bottom, which is made up of very smooth rock, are small Diptera larvae, which resist the pull of the current by attaching themselves to the rocks by means of six ventricle suckers. The only fish that lives in this environment is the bullhead.

Mountain torrents

There are a lot of rapids and waterfalls, the bottom is made up of large rocks or living rock. Salmonidae (the trout belongs to this family) are typical of these waters.

On the river bed of these waters, the insect larvae of the Plecoptera are found, usually under the rocks. These, like the salmonids, need pure water that is rich in oxygen, to live. The legs of Plecoptera are equipped with little hooks which allow them to resist the current. The aquatic vegetation is very scarce and is made up mainly of blue algae which grow on the surface of rocks, making them slippery. Along the banks of the river there are usually coniferous forests.

At the foot of the mountain

The river at the foot of the mountain is deep and the bed is made up of pebbles and small stones. The reason for this is that as the river descends to the valley, the current decreases in speed allowing the deposit of smaller material on the bottom and the banks to settle.

Among the many organisms present are an abundance of insect larvae which include the insect orders Plecoptera, Ephemeroptera and Trichoptera.

The most characteristic fish is the barbel, so called because of the presence of barbs on its chin. Along the banks are many water-loving trees, especially willows, growing either singly or in groups.

Bullhead

Trout

Barbel

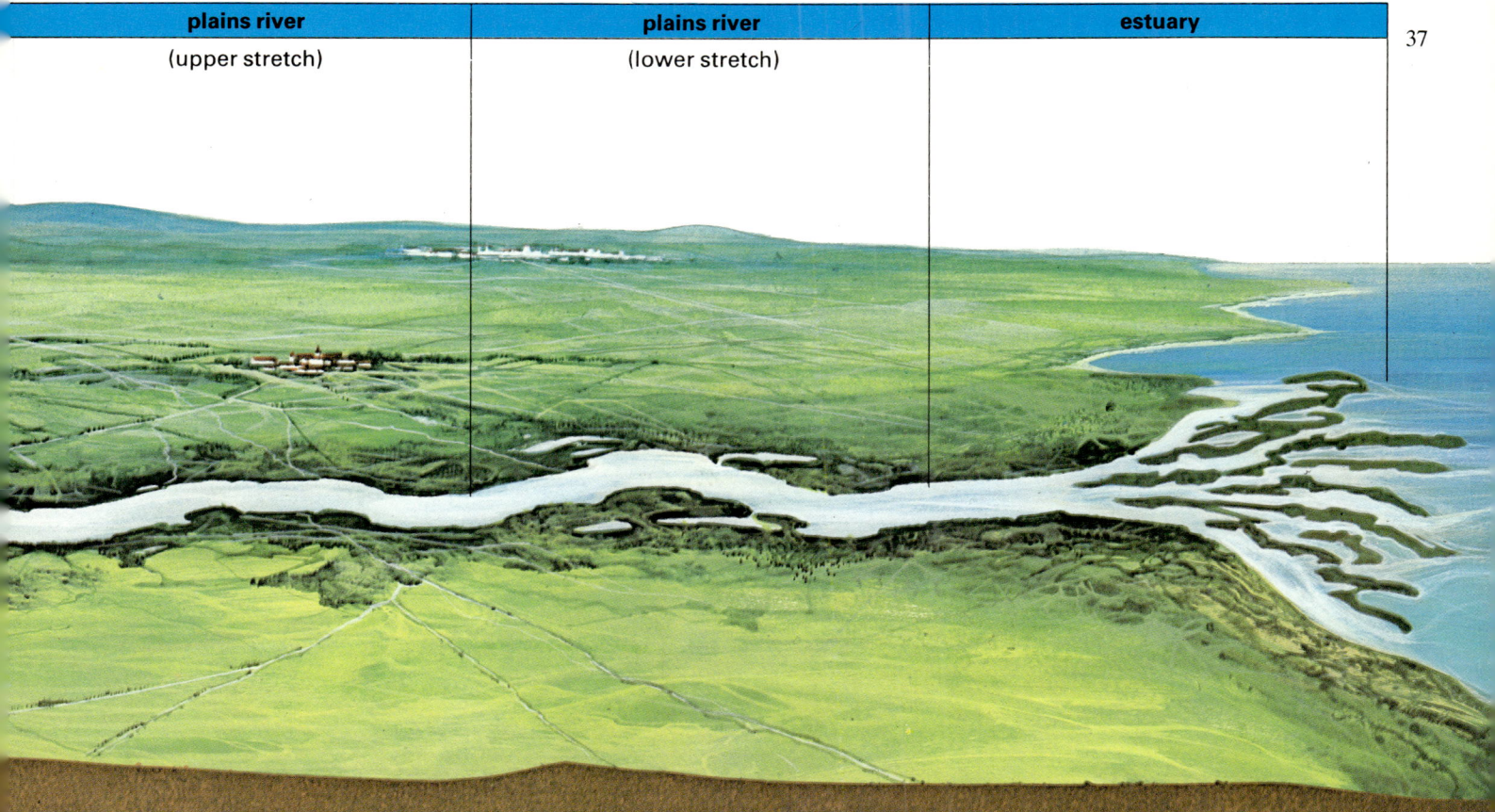

sand and pebbles	lime and sand	lime

The plains river
Two stretches can be distinguished, the upper and the lower. In the upper stretch the bottom and the banks are made up mostly of sand and the river moves more slowly. In the lower stretch, the bottom and the banks are usually made up of lime and the river meanders with gentle curves. There are sometimes many marshes here.

In the latter stretch, living organisms are similar to those found in still water. That is, those capable of thriving in water with a low oxygen content and a high temperature. Among invertebrates there is an abundance of oligochaete worms, bivalvular molluscs, water snails, sponges, insect larvae (mosquito and dragonflies) and also adult insects such as Coleoptera.

There are more fish species than in the previous stretches and the largest family present is that of the Cyprinidae. The most characteristic species of the upper stretches is the chub and that of the lower stretches is the tench. The most widespread plants are reeds. Along the banks of the river are meadows and cultivated fields.

The carp, another common river fish, was introduced into the United States during the last century and took to river life in the warm, southern states so successfully that native fish and aquatic vegetation suffered. The carp originally came from the watershed of the Caspian and Black Seas and has spread over Europe, much to the pleasure of anglers to whom the fish gives great sport, so much so that carp are specially bred

in ponds and lakes, and when the fish are adult they are released into fishing rivers.

The estuary
At the river mouth, the mixture of fresh water and salt water from the sea creates a special environment, in which the animals have to be able to withstand changes in the salt content due to the tides and the variations in the volume of the river. There are very few species which can live in this environment, but among them is a little shrimp from the family Palaemonidae and a small fish of the Cyprinidae family, which is called a sea-snail. River mouths are often used by sea fish. For some this is temporary but others, such as the mullet, spend some time there each year.

Chub   **Tench**   **Sea-snail**

Look but do not touch! This is the silent message given out by the butterfly fish. If an unsuspecting admirer was drawn by its beauty and tried to catch it, he would be badly poisoned by a sting hidden among the elegant fins. And this is only one example of looks being deceptive. The world of sea fish holds an infinite number of surprises. Some are peaceful surface feeders, others are vicious predators that feed on other fish and mammals much larger than themselves.

THE LARGEST 'CONTINENT'?

Life on our planet originated in the sea more than three billion years ago.

Still, today, this endless liquid continent occupies a surface area equal to twice that of dry land and holds an extremely rich fauna which is much more varied than that of dry land. Representatives of all animal types can be found in the sea, whilst only seven can be found on dry land.

For hundreds of millions of years, fish have dominated this submerged continent.

It was under the seas that the first life appeared on Earth during pre-Cambrian times. These first animals were the trilobites, gastropods, bivalves, molluscs, sponges and brachiopods that we know a great deal about because of the fossils that have been discovered around the world.

The underwater world

The surface of the sea is monotonous and uniform but its dull appearance hides an exceptional variety of environments – coastal waters, with sandy or rocky bottoms rich in ravines and covered with thick vegetation; the endless spaces of the open seas; the dark depths of the abysses where plant life is absent and the water pressure is unbelievable – but all these places are home to the assortment of fish in the sea.

Among the rocks of the shallows can be found fat, sedentary fish of very varied colours. In the open sea the fish are very different: they are all similar in appearance with a shape adapted to pushing through the water with the greatest possible speed. Their colour does not vary much, being either grey or blue on the back and white or

Fish of the Sea

silver on the belly. This is to camouflage the fish in the vast body of water. Fish which live near the surface of the open seas are called pelagic fish, and they include species which are very important to the human economy because they often move about in enormous shoals which can be fished in large quantities.

The old saying, 'there are more fish in the sea than ever came out of it' may no longer be true. Overfishing of 'commercial' breeds have depleted the stocks of many species of fish. Twentieth-century technology has enabled trawlermen to locate the fish and catch them in ever-increasing quantities. This has become a cause of great concern to the governments of countries where fishing is a major industry. In the North Sea, the herring on which British and Scandinavian trawlermen depend for their livelihood have become so seriously depleted that quotas have been introduced. Similarly, overfishing of salmon at sea has caused a great decrease in the numbers of these magnificent fish that come up river to spawn.

There are also fish which live in the depths of the ocean, commonly called abyssal fish. These animals can live several thousand metres below the surface and

Above, a dense school of young herring and on the opposite page, a butterfly fish.

their environment is cold and dark. In the endless darkness in which they live, they recognise each other by a faint light which they emit from special organs. The abyssal zone, and its luminous creatures with their ghost-like aspect, is a world that man has only recently begun to explore and which certainly holds many more surprises.

THREE LIFESTYLES
There are about 150 families of fish but in order to understand them better, three families are described here. They are the Clupeida which live in the open seas; the Scorpaenidae, most species of which live in coastal water, and the Chauliodontidae which live in the deep waters of the sea.

Clupeidae, pelagic fish
The fish which is caught more than any other is the herring, which belongs to the family of Clupeidae. Other species which

A viper fish (Chauliodus sloanei) *from the Chauliodontidae family.*

are important to the human economy also belong to the same family. These are the sardine and the sprat. All of these species live in the open sea and are usually united in enormous schools. They usually eat planktonic animals such as crustaceans, mollusc larvae and fry (newly born fish).

Scorpaenidae, coastal fish
Although they are known to go down to depths of from two to four hundred metres, the scorponids are typical coastal fish. The scorpion fish is common in the waters of the Mediterranean where it lives camouflaged among the rocks by a special 'tint' and the appendages it has on its nose which look like tiny algae. Hidden among the rocks, the scorpion fish ambushes its prey. Therefore, the fact that it swims very slowly is not a disadvantage to it. To defend itself from predators, in addition to its camouflage, the scorpion fish also has poisonous glands underneath its dorsal fins which are capable of giving a nasty sting. Even more dangerous are some tropical species of the family such as the butterfly fish.

Chauliodontidae, abyssal fish
Chauliodontids are also called viper fish. They are typical creatures of the marine abysses. Along their sides they have two rows of special light-emitting organs and their large mouths have long curved teeth. The chauliodontids live during the day at depths of from one to three thousand metres, but at night they move to shallower water where food is more abundant. Like almost all abyssal fish, the Chauliodontidae are voracious predators which swallow their victims in one gulp.

1. **Mackerel** (*Scomber scombus*): a pelagic fish from the Atlantic and the Mediterranean.
2. **Flying fish** (*Cypselurus heterurus*): abundant in the Atlantic and able to glide over the water using their highly developed pectoral fins.
3. **Herring** (*Clupea harengus*): the most abundant pelagic fish in the Atlantic.
4. **Sail-fish** (*Istiophorus platypterus*): a large pelagic fish from the Atlantic similar to the sword fish. Probably the fastest of all fish.

5. **Mackerel shark** (*Carcharhinus sp.*): is found in the Mediterranean.
6. **Remora** (*Echeneis naucrates*): because of a sucker on its back, this fish sticks itself to the stomach of other fish.
7. **Pilot-fish** (*Naucrates ductor*): usually called this because it has the habit of preceding large sharks.
8. **Angler fish** (*Lophius piscatorius*): it lives on the seabed and attracts the little fish it eats by waving around the appendages on its head.
9. **Greater weever fish** (*Trachinus draco*):

it has poisonous spines positioned on the dorsal fin.
10. **Sole** (*Solea solea*): a typical seabed fish, it has a flat body and is a blotchy brown colour.
11. **Tuna** (*Thunnus thynnus*): these large pelagic fish move about in big schools which make them very economic to catch.
12. **Scorpion-fish** (*Scorpaena sp.*): this Mediterranean species is a typical coastal fish.
13. **Surgeon-fish** (*Acanthurus sp.*): this beautiful species is common in the Pacific Ocean around coral islands.

14. Squirrel-fish (*Holocentrus xantherythrus*): this tropical species is best known for the strength of its spines.

15. Barracuda (*Sphyraena barracuda*): after sharks, these are the most feared of all predatory fish. They live in tropical seas.

16. Grouper (*Epinephelus sp.*): related to the cernias of domestic waters, which have beautiful bright colours.

17. Clown fish (*Amphiprion percula*): because of its bright colours, it is able to camouflage itself in the corals.

18. Rock mullet (*Mullus surmuletus*):

recognisable by the barb on its chin.

19. Sardine (*Sardina pilchardus*): after the herring this is the most common pelagic fish in the Atlantic.

20. Manta ray (*Manta hamiltoni*): in spite of its threatening look, this huge cartilaginous ray fish is harmless.

21. Trigger fish (*Balistes vetula*): this species and others like it are common among the corals of tropical shallows.

22. Puffer (*Lagocophelus lacrigatus*): called this because when it is threatened it puffs itself up into a ball-shape.

23. Angel-fish (*Heniochus acuminatus*): because of their beauty, angel-fish are kept in aquariums.

24. Pomacanth (*Pomacanthus sp.*): the best known representative of the widespread tropical family of pomacantids.

25. Spotted moray eel (*Gymnothorax faragineus*): the bite of this species, like that of the better known common moray eel, is very poisonous.

26. Yellow angel-fish (*Forcipiger longirostris*): a species characterised by the unusual length of its nose.

BONY FISH AND CARTILAGINOUS FISH

There are two main groups of fish. The first is the group called 'teleost' fish. They are commonly called 'bony' fish. The other group consists of the cartilaginous fish. The teleost group contains the vast majority of fish which includes nearly all of those already described. The cartilaginous group is much smaller and includes the ray fish.

The best known cartilaginous fish are sharks, the most feared marine predators. The largest of the sharks is the whale shark which can reach a length of 18 metres or more. Despite its size, it is quite harmless. Cartilaginous fish belong to races and species which are close to each other. These are flat fish which usually move around on the sand or muddy seabed. There are also very large species of flat fish among this group, such as the manta ray shown on the previous page (number 20).

WAYS TO OBSERVE FISH

There are many ways of observing sea fish and they are all good fun. Here are some of them.

The easiest way . . .

Go to a fish market. The fresh fish can be recognised by their bright colours and firm flesh. It is easy to find out which fish are

Tropical fish swimming among the rocks of a coral reef in the waters round the Maldive Islands (Indian Ocean).

THE STRANGEST FISH

It is not true that all fish look like each other. Take, for example, the seahorse. Unlike all other fish, it has an elongated nose and neck and a tail which looks as though it should belong to some other animal. Moreover, the body of the seahorse has no scales. The seahorse also moves in an upright position, which is totally different from other fish. Only by observing it very closely can it be discovered that it is a fish. Adult sea horses can be from 4 to 30 cm in length.

The seahorse belongs to the family Syngnathidae which also contains other strange species such as the needle fish, or the leaf fish of Australia, which is well camouflaged by its strange, leaf-like flaps of skin. Seahorses are able to grip on to plants by using their tails. Another strange thing about this fish is that it is the male who gets pregnant. The female fills the male's pouch with eggs and it is he who actually gives birth!

Another strange fish is the photocorynus. The male is a fraction of the size of the female and lives permanently attached to her. He latches on by his mouth to a special protuberance just above her snout and feeds from her; in return, he supplies her with the sperm that she needs to fertilise her eggs.

Leaf fish

Seahorse

Needle fish

common and which are rare – the cheaper the fish, usually the more easy it is to catch. More expensive fish are usually much rarer.

. . . The nicest way . . .

Is to swim in the sea near the shore using a snorkel tube and mask. By moving slowly over rock or sandy bottom it is possible to make interesting observations about fish. This way of looking at fish is perfect for getting to know them better. By studying them in their natural environment, it is possible to note their behaviour patterns, their swimming speed and many other important details.

. . . The most adventurous way . . .

Is to go on board a fishing boat and participate in a fishing expedition. When the nets are pulled aboard, they are full of fish of many types that would be impossible to see by swimming, as they live in deeper waters; or from going to a fish market, for some of the fish on board would not be edible and therefore, not in the market. A lot of secrets about fish can be learned from fishermen. Fishing folk know a lot and often love telling stories.

ENDANGERED SPECIES

As if fish have not enough to cope with from natural predators in the sea, and man's sophisticated fishing techniques, the threat of pollution is a major danger. Hardly a year goes by without our newspapers carrying banner headlines telling of an oil tanker breaking up and disgorging its cargo of crude oil into the sea in the form of suffocating oil slicks which kill or damage any fish unfortunate enough to swim through it. The slick also kills the plankton on which so many of the fish feed.

Another major threat comes from care-

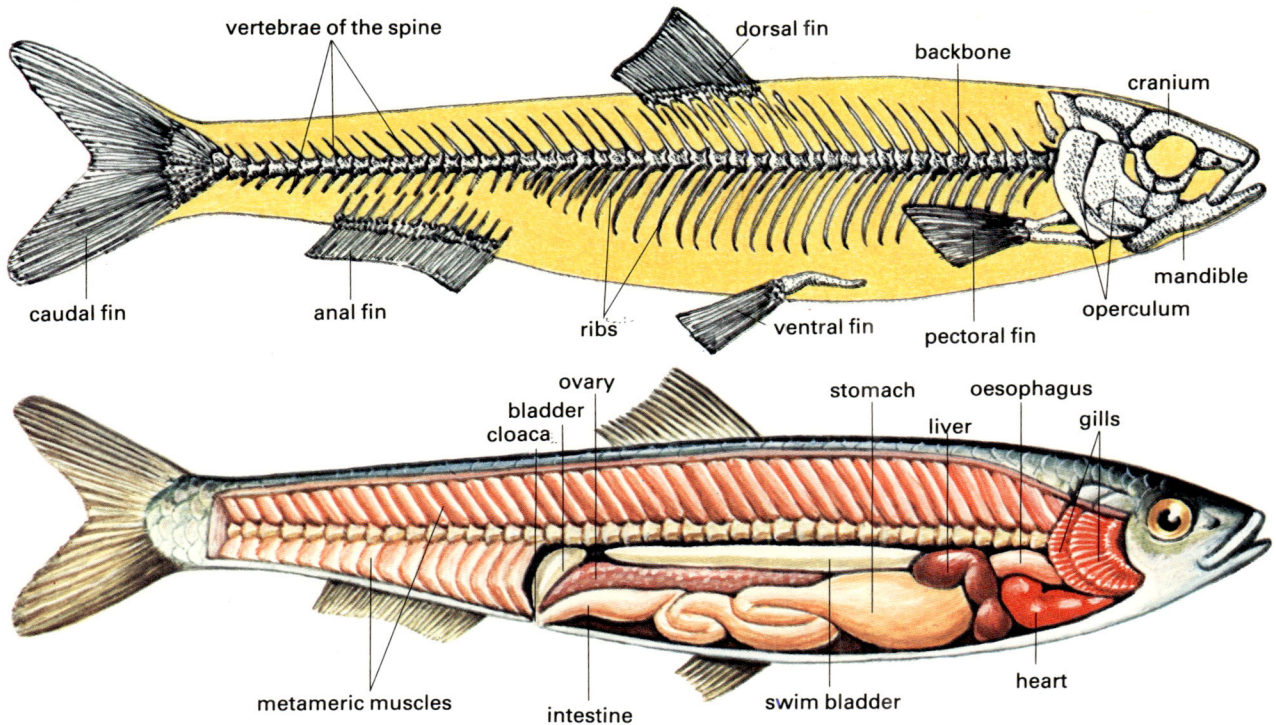

vertebrae of the spine
dorsal fin
backbone
cranium
caudal fin
anal fin
ribs
ventral fin
pectoral fin
mandible
operculum

ovary
bladder
cloaca
stomach
oesophagus
liver
gills
metameric muscles
intestine
swim bladder
heart

Anatomy of a sardine

less dumping of industrial effluent and sewage into rivers and seas around the world. Not only are many fish killed directly by this poison, but others breed mutant offspring. In Japan this is a particularly serious problem – many of the fish that swim the coastal waters being so poisonous that if eaten by humans the results can be fatal.

THE STRUCTURE OF THE FISH

It is not hard to discover how a fish is made up. One only has to watch a fish being gutted prior to cooking to learn about its anatomy. A typical example is the sardine, known to us in its adult form as the pilchard.

From the outside the fish has three uneven fins (caudal, anal and dorsal) and two pairs of even fins (pectoral and ventral). Its gills are protected by a sort of bony shield called the operculum. Inside the body there are several organs which are familiar in human anatomy, such as the brain (although not very highly developed); the stomach; the intestine; the liver; the bladder and the heart. The heart of the sardine is not divided into four cavities as in mammals, but only into two (an atrium and a ventricle). The fish has no lungs. All the respiratory work is done by the gills. In addition, the fish has an organ called the swim bladder which enables it to float, and which is lacking in land vertebrates. (Zoologists are of the opinion that our lungs evolved over millions of years from the swim bladder of fish.) A simple look at its skeletal and muscular apparatus shows how perfectly the fish is adapted for life in the water.

The biological cycle
Sardines are extremely prolific breeders and every female lays thousands of eggs each year. Yet the number of sardines in the sea does not tend to increase greatly from one year to the next, but rather to decrease due to over-intensive fishing by man to satisfy the seemingly insatiable demand for sardines in many countries of the world.

This sketch shows how sardines are preyed upon at various stages of development so that, although a large number of eggs are laid by the adults, the total number of fish

The smaller fish are usually sent to canning factories, the larger ones are sold fresh.

The eggs, left to themselves, are devoured in huge quantities by other fish and the same thing happens to their fry. Even adults are preyed on by other fish so that in the end the total number of pilchards does not change very much, despite the vast numbers of eggs laid.

does not change very much. The sketch is simplified so that the total number of eggs and fry in relation to the number of adults is less than it would be in reality.

The biological cycle of the sardine

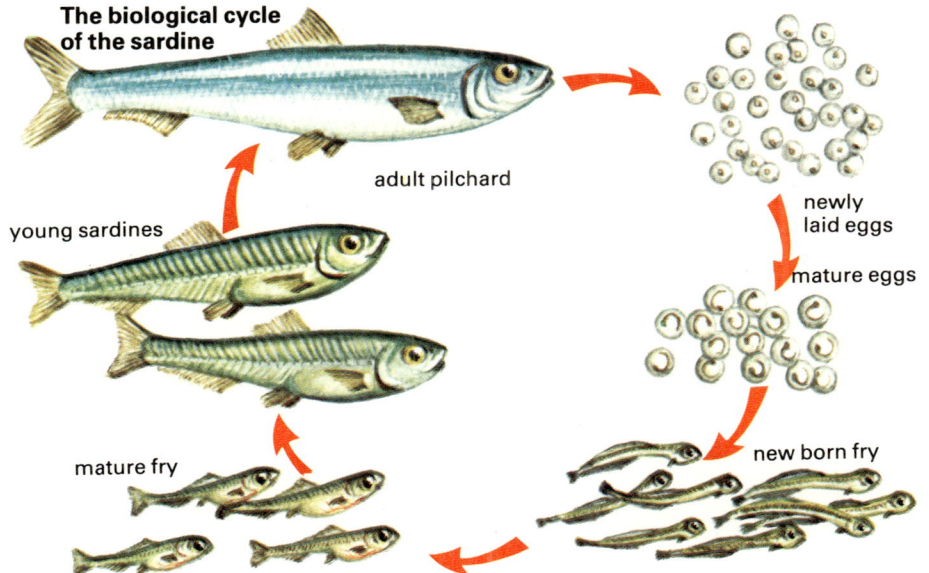

adult pilchard
young sardines
newly laid eggs
mature eggs
mature fry
new born fry

All over the world wherever there is water, there are fishes living in it. Fishes are the masters of the underwater world. For more than 360 million years they have inhabited it. Many live at sea, but there are more than 8,000 species of freshwater fishes which spend their lives in lakes, ponds, fast-flowing rivers and meandering streams. From the mighty salmon to the tiny minnow, the world of freshwater fish is one of endless fascination.

On these pages we have illustrated some of the fishes that are commonly found in the fresh waters of Europe.

1. River lamprey (*Lampetra fluviatilis*): a sea fish that swims up rivers to spawn. It is a parasitic fish, attaching itself to an unfortunate victim and living off the blood and body juices that it sucks in.

2. Lake trout (*Salmo lacustris*): a large cousin of the brown trout. It grows to between 60 and 80 centimetres in length.

3. Chub (*Leuciscus cephalus*): lives in slow-running water, living off small water animals and vegetation.

4. Sturgeon (*Acipenser sturio*): lives at sea and comes up river to spawn. It can grow up to three metres in length. Its eggs are the luxury food caviare.

5. Bream (*Abramis brama*): commonly found in slow-running waters in Europe. It grows up to 60 centimetres in length.

6. Three-spined stickleback (*Gasterosteus aculeatus*): a small fish that lives both in the sea and in fresh water. The male (shown here) sports these bright colours only during courtship. They swim with short spurts of speed and then pause.

7. Black bullhead catfish (*Ictalarus melas*): Originally came from North America but is now common in Europe.

Freshwater Fish

8. Perch *(Perca fluviatilis): swift, bottom-dwelling fish. Common in European lakes and fast-flowing rivers.*
9. Carp *(Cyprinus carpio): lives in lowland lakes and river backwaters. It grubs for its food along the bed. Some carp are said to live for fifty years.*
10. Bleak *(Alburnus alburnus): small fish common in slow running waters.*
11. Northern pike *(Esox lucius): voracious predator, it grows up to 1.3 metres in length.*
12. Grayling *(Thymallus thymallus): much prized by anglers, the grayling lives in deep, fast-flowing rivers.*

13. Pumpkinseed *(Lepomis gibbosus): originally found in North America, now common through Europe.*
14. Freshwater eel *(Anguilla anguilla): lives in rivers and swims far out into the Atlantic Ocean to spawn.*
15. Pikeperch *(Lucioperca lucioperca): particularly common in lowland lakes and large rivers where it lives in clouded waters.*
16. Loach *(Cobitus taenia): usually lives in still waters.*
17. Salmon *(Salmo salar): swims upriver to spawn making spectacular leaps as it goes. Anglers pay huge sums of money for the privilege of fishing for them.*

SMALL BUT DEADLY

In the rivers of Central and South America there lives a little fish that is one of the most aggressive of all fishes. The savage habits of the piranha have become almost legendary. There are many stories of the speed with which a school of them can strip the body of an unfortunate animal, which has slipped into the water, down to its bones in a matter of seconds. Its teeth are razor sharp and the merest trace of blood in the water will send a school of them into a wild frenzy. Usually the piranha feeds on small fish and is not averse to eating other piranha. Surprisingly, larger piranhas give local fisherman good sport and with their white, firm flesh are good to eat.

FROM FRESH WATER TO THE SEA. . . .

The conditions in which fish have to live at sea and in fresh water are so completely different that it is difficult for freshwater fish to live in the sea and for sea fish to live in fresh water. Difficult, but not impossible.

The mullet, for example, is a sea fish which quite often swims upriver where feeding conditions are easier than they are at sea. Other fish, for example the salmon and the eel, live for parts of their lives in the sea and for other, quite distinct, parts of their lives in fresh water.

Eels live for most of their lives in rivers and lakes all over Europe. When they are between seven and twelve years of age (depending on feeding conditions) they migrate down river to the sea – well-nourished eels leave sooner.

With short interruptions the eels swim for about fifteen kilometres each day, and when they reach the sea they head west into the Atlantic Ocean and carry on swimming until they reach the Sargasso Sea, where they spawn.

Young eel larvae are quite unlike the adult fish. Their bodies are leaf-shaped and transparent. They are carried along by the warm waters of the Gulf Stream and when they are about three years old (by which time they are eight to ten centimetres long) they gather in their millions off the Continental Shelf. Here they are transformed into transparent, cylindrical 'glass eels'. They begin to move inshore, becoming less transparent and more pigmented as they swim, until, as elvers, they swim up the estuaries of our rivers in the so-called 'Elver run'. They live in the rivers until it is time for them to take the same journey that the previous generation of eels did so many years before. It is a journey from which adult eels never return. No one knows what the eventual fate of the eels is once they have spawned. No silver eel (the term for adult eels on their journey to spawn) has ever been caught in the Ocean on a return journey home. And none has ever been known to return to their rivers after spawning. However adult eels kept in captivity have been known to live for ninety years.

. . . and the other way round

The life cycle of the salmon is exactly opposite to that of the eel. Salmon are born in rivers and live at sea until it is time for them to return to the same river where they were spawned to spawn themselves when they are mature fish. Salmon will stop at nothing to return to their home waters. They will swim against raging torrents and leap over any obstacles in their way. Leaps of three or four metres are not uncommon. On rivers where hydro-electric stations have been built which obstruct salmon runs, special waterways have been built to aid the salmon to continue their journey.

No one has yet fathomed out how the salmon find their way back to their home rivers. It is one of the mysteries of nature that defies explanation.

When it comes up river to spawn, the salmon is a magnificent fish. Its flesh is firm and pink, its skin is silver and its body is strong and muscular. Anglers pay large sums of money to buy the fishing rights in salmon rivers because adult salmon give such good sport to the angler.

Spawning takes place on gravelly and stony riverbeds. The female makes a nest by jerking her tail backwards and forwards and deposits her eggs in it. She usually lays anything from four to twenty thousand eggs at a time, but half of these go unfertilised and few of those that are fertilised hatch. When they are fertilised, the female covers the eggs with sand.

Most salmon make the journey to their spawning grounds only once in their lives and die immediately afterwards. Those who survive to swim back to the open sea usually die of exhaustion or disease shortly after their return.

The young hatch in the spring and live in their rivers or streams for from one to five

The development of the eel

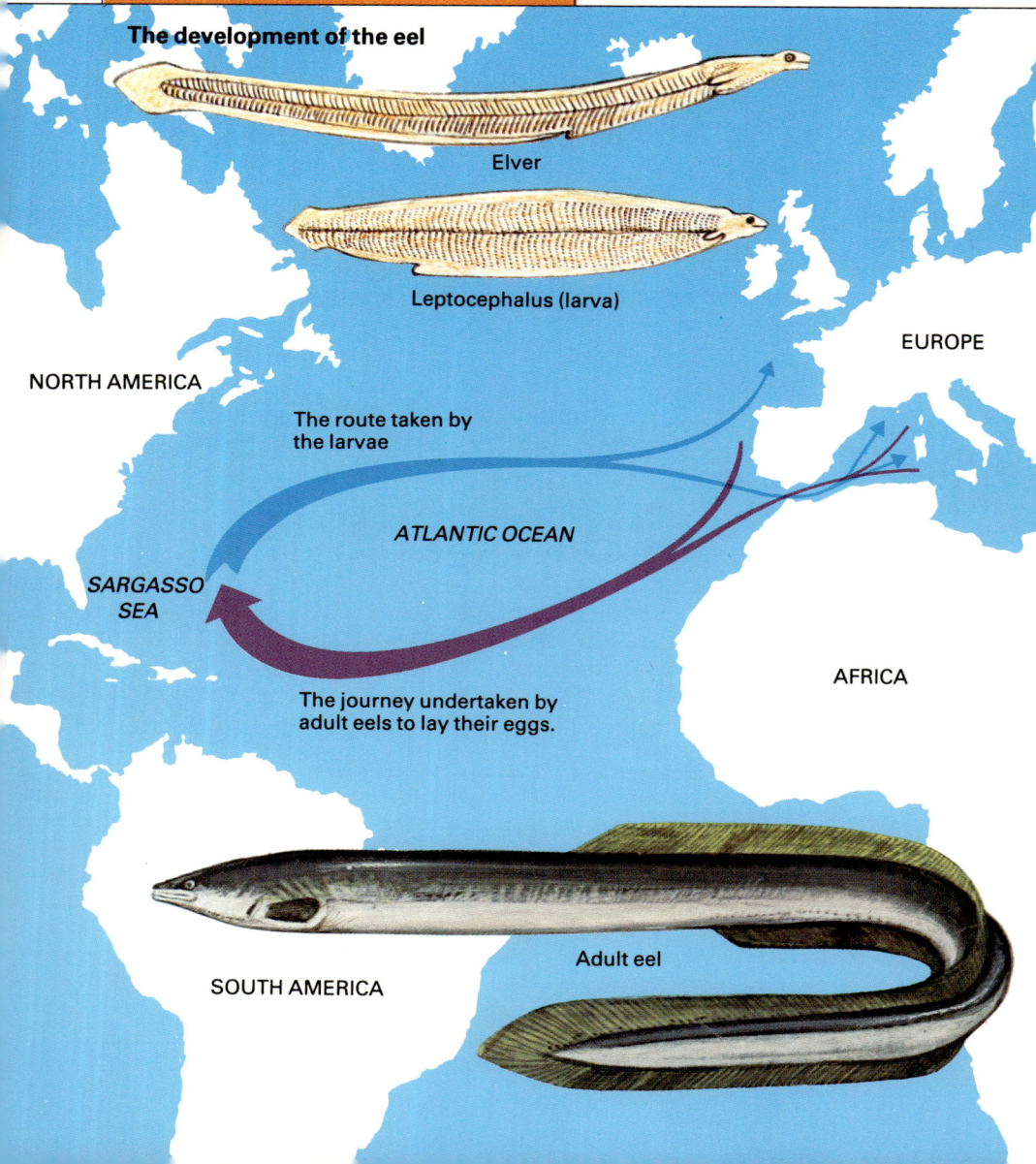

Elver

Leptocephalus (larva)

NORTH AMERICA

The route taken by the larvae

ATLANTIC OCEAN

SARGASSO SEA

EUROPE

AFRICA

The journey undertaken by adult eels to lay their eggs.

SOUTH AMERICA

Adult eel

Sea fish are usually much larger than freshwater fish as shown here.

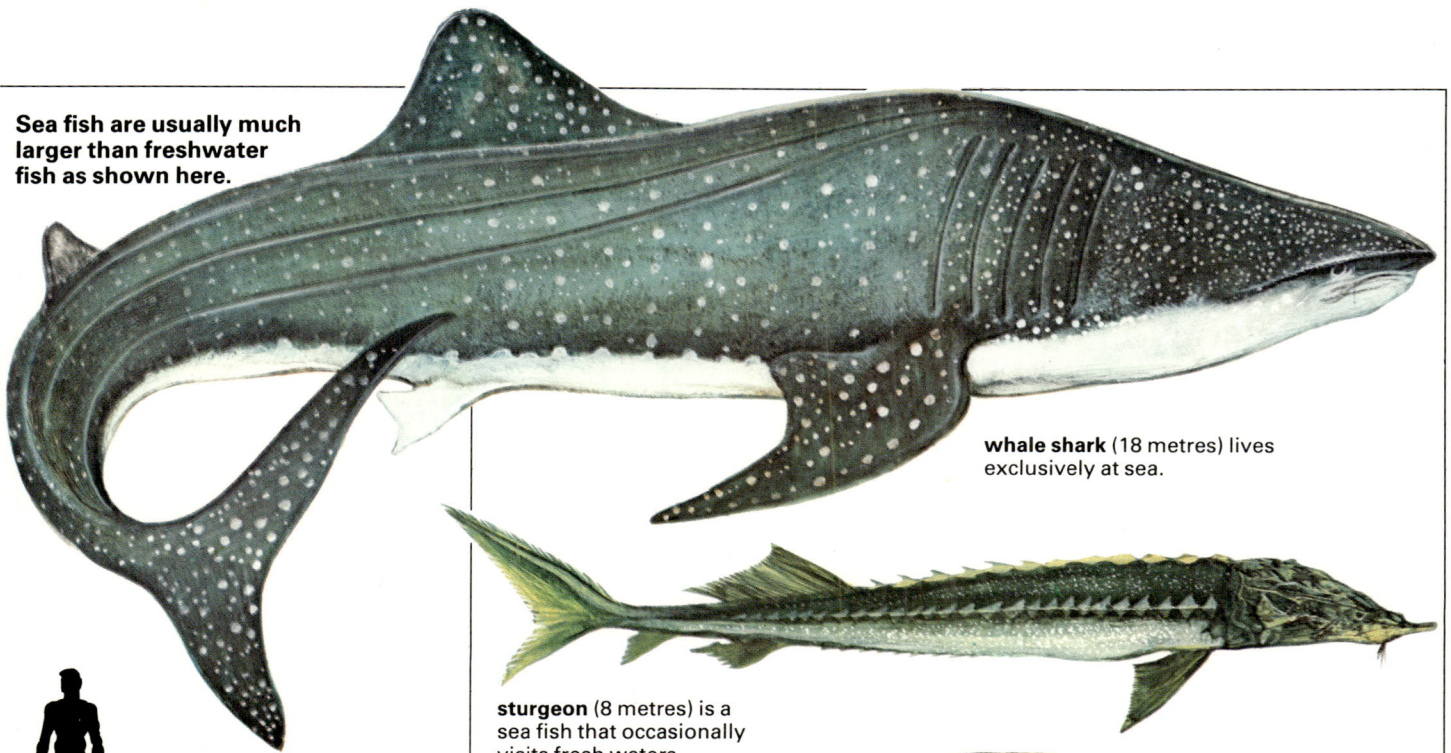

whale shark (18 metres) lives exclusively at sea.

A man drawn to the same scale as the fish illustrated here.

sturgeon (8 metres) is a sea fish that occasionally visits fresh waters.

arapaima (5 metres) lives exclusively in fresh water.

years during which time they are known as parrs. When the parr phase is over, the young fish, now known as smolt, swim down to the sea where they find abundant food, particularly herring, and grow very quickly to their full size and weight (usually up to one-and-a half metres and up to 40 kilogrammes). After two or three years in the sea the salmon return to their native breeding ground to spawn and, usually, to die, only a few surviving to swim down river and back to the open sea again.

It is at this stage in their lives, as the fish swim up-river, that salmon are usually caught by anglers. It gives great sport and is delicious to eat. It is rightly called 'the king of fish'.

SEA AND FRESH WATER FISH

Zoologists do not think of sea fish and freshwater fish as distinct groups, but there are differences between the two caused by the different environments in which they live.

One important difference is that freshwater fish are rarely as brightly coloured as their sea cousins. They are normally dull brown or grey with dark speckled spots on their bodies. In a few freshwater species the male is more brightly coloured than the female.

Young freshwater fish are miniature versions of the adult fish, unlike many sea fish who go through a series of metamorphoses before they begin to look like adult fish (just like the eels we looked at on the previous page which go through many stages in their

amazingly long swim from the Sargasso Sea to the rivers of Europe).

Freshwater fish never grow to the same lengths as sea fish. The longest freshwater fish in the world is the arapaima which is found in the River Amazon in South America. It can grow to five metres. The largest sea fish, the Whale shark, can grow to up to eighteen metres in length!

Even fresh waters have a small amount of salt in them and this can seep through the fish's skin and cause it harm. It has to be expelled and to do so the freshwater fish pass out a small quantity of salt on their urine. Sea fish, on the other hand, take in a great deal more salt and their urine is much saltier – often more than five times as salty as a freshwater fish's.

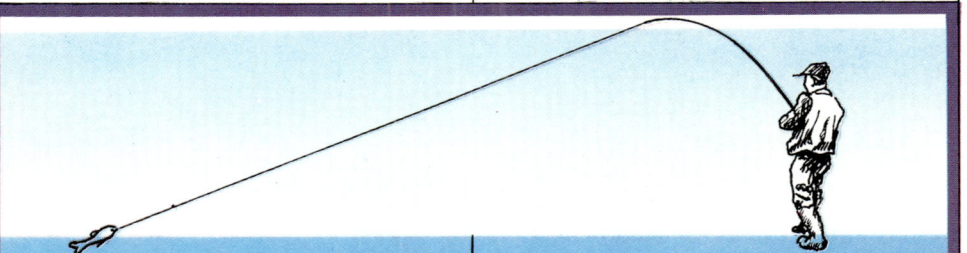

LET'S GO FISHING

We are very lucky in this country to have so many rivers, streams, ponds and lakes which we can fish. Angling is the most popular participant sport in the United Kingdom – it is also one of the most enjoyable.

If you wish to take up fishing as a hobby there is sure to be a sports shop near you that will sell you inexpensive fishing tackle.

The basic fishing tackle is a hook, a line and a pole. There is a vast difference between simple canal fishing and sophisticated salmon fishing that involves much more expensive equipment, and a great deal of money to pay for the rights to fish the usually privately-owned waters.

You must always make sure that you have

the necessary permission before you fish a water. Some local authorities insist that anglers have a licence before they are allowed to fish in their waters. Don't be alarmed. They are easy to obtain and cost only a few pence.

If you want to fish a private stretch of water or privately owned lake, you must ask the owner's permission.

Find out if there is an angling club near you. If there is, do not hesitate to join it. Not only is it fun to fish alongside friends, but these clubs often organise outings to rivers and lakes some distance away that you may not be able to get to under your own steam. Have fun.

INDEX

PRINTED IN BELGIUM BY
proost
INTERNATIONAL BOOK PRODUCTION

84   C-34